Pocket Full of
Christmas

Pocket Full of Christmas

Having a Purpose Filled Advent

Cheryle M. Touchton

Pleasant Word
A Division of WINEPRESS PUBLISHING

Pleasant Word (a division of WinePress Publishing, PO Box 428, Enumclaw, WA 98022) functions only as book publisher. As such, the ultimate design, content, editorial accuracy, and views expressed or implied in this work are those of the author.

Unless otherwise noted, all Scriptures are taken from the Holy Bible, New International Version, Copyright © 1973, 1978, 1984 by the International Bible Society. Used by permission of Zondervan Publishing House. The "NIV" and "New International Version" trademarks are registered in the United States Patent and Trademark Office by International Bible Society.

Scripture references marked KJV are taken from the King James Version of the Bible.

Scripture references marked NASB are taken from the New American Standard Bible, © 1960, 1963, 1968, 1971, 1972, 1973, 1975, 1977 by The Lockman Foundation. Used by permission.

Scripture references marked AMP are taken from The Amplified Bible, Old Testament, © 1965 and 1987 by The Zondervan Corporation, and from The Amplified New Testament, © 1954, 1958, 1987 by The Lockman Foundation.   Used by permission.

Scripture references marked TMB are taken from The Message Bible © 1993 by Eugene N. Peterson, NavPress, POB 35001, Colorado Springs, CO 80935, 4th printing in USA 1994. Published in association with the literary agency—Aline Comm. POB 49068, Colorado Springs, CO 80949. Used by permission

ISBN 1-4141-0486-3
Library of Congress Catalog Card Number: 2005903978

Dedication

This book is lovingly dedicated to my husband, Bob, who makes all my Christmases special. It is also dedicated to my Sunday School teachers, Jim and Linda Gandy, who have encouraged the publication of this work and my ministry. Everyone should aspire to their model for Christian living. Special thanks go to Michelle LaMontagne for her love and support in editing.

Table of Contents

Introduction

Dear Readers:

I love the sights, sounds, smells, and feelings of Christmas. The music reminds me of the angels singing on that first Christmas morning. Worship services prompt gratitude for God's precious gift to everyone who chooses to unwrap it. Family celebrations offer time to gather and love others with the love of Christ. Whiffs of cinnamon, evergreen, and peppermint remind me of the glory of God's creation. Gift giving allows us to lay gifts at the feet of the Christ Child. Everywhere, God reminds us that He came to earth as a baby.

I didn't always love Christmas. There was a time when I saw Christmas through jaded eyes. I complained that Christmas had lost its meaning due to retailers looking to increase revenue through commercialization, the pressure of having to buy gifts for demanding people, and the exhaustion created by the time pressures of the season. I grumbled my way through malls, parties, worship services, gift wrapping, and putting up decorations. When Christmas was over, I collapsed, bemoaning the staggering bills that began to arrive.

One Christmas, in the middle of my whining, a friend challenged me to look for the true meaning of Christmas. "You don't seem to enjoy anything about Christmas," she accused. Horrified, I realized it wasn't Christmas that had lost its meaning. I was the one who had lost Christ in the middle of the noise, chaos, and abundance of the season. I fell to my knees in confession.

All of a sudden, I had a Pocket Full of Christmas. As I started seeking Christ in Christmas, Jesus demonstrated that He is everywhere. Walking through the malls, I heard His carols. I noticed advertising and saw Christ in the word Christmas. Instead of seeing greedy retailers, I began to see a clever God using these unknowing retailers to spread His message. As I prayed about gift giving, each gift became a gift to the Christ child. As I prepared for family celebrations, I understood that by cooking and preparing for the people of Jesus, I was doing it for Him. I saw how my bitterness had kept me from organizing my activities so I had time for Christ.

As I began asking God for knowledge of His will and the power to carry it out, God began orchestrating my Christmas celebrations so that every event was a tribute to Him. Christmas is now my favorite time of the year.

As Christians, we know *the* purpose of Christmas. Sometimes the difficulties and busyness of the holidays keep us from pursuing *our* purpose in the Christmas season. Demons such as exhaustion, discouragement, and loneliness become powerful tools of Satan for depleting our pockets as we scurry through malls, hurriedly wrap gifts, lament about finances, and remember the people no longer with us. *Pocket Full of Christmas* will help us refocus and go through this Christmas season finding Christ in each Christmas celebration.

A gift opens the way for the giver and ushers us into the presence of the great (Proverbs 18:16). At Christmas, we give gifts to the Holy Christ Child by giving gifts to each other (Matthew 25:40). *Pocket Full of Christmas* is a gift to be unwrapped each day of Advent, beginning on December 1 with each session taking between 30-45 minutes. You will need your Bible and a pen.

These devotions are designed to help you spiritually and organizationally during this busiest time of the year. Each day contains a meditation, a Bible Study, an application exercise, and an organizational exercise. There are daily instructions for how to use the four Appendices that are located at the end of the book.

- Appendix A: Requests of the Christ Child – A **prayer list** for documenting Christmas prayer requests and answers
- Appendix B: Gifts from the Christ Child – A **gratitude list** for documenting Christmas blessings
- Appendix C: Gifts to the Christ Child – A **gift list** for planning, budgeting, and recording gifts to others
- Appendix D: Celebrations for the Christ Child – A **"To Do" list** for organizing Christmas activities so you can enjoy your Christmas events and celebrations

As Christians, we serve God in our worshiping, shopping, wrapping, cleaning, decorating, and cooking. With the right attitude and preparation, each action we take in preparation for Christmas can be an act of obedience and love as we celebrate Christ's birth. We each choose the spirit in which we serve. "Full pockets" is a metaphor for being prepared. My prayer for you this Christmas is that you fill your pockets with the Spirit of Christ. I look forward to spending Christmas with you.

Blessings,
Cheryle M. Touchton
Pocket Full of Change Ministries

Godly Fellowship at Christmas

Meditation (3-5 Minutes)

Begin by being still before God. Meditate on the words "Be still, and know that I am God; I will be exalted among the nations, I will be exalted in the earth." (Psalm 46:10 NIV)

- Be still.
  - Clear your mind.
  - Breathe deeply.
  - Sit quietly.
- Know He is God.
  - Feel His presence.
  - Let His presence envelop you.
  - He is exalted among the nations and on the earth.
- Feel His power.
  - Surrender to His power.
  - Realize that He will be exalted among the nations this Christmas.
  - Claim His power.
- Listen to the voice of God.

Prayer (5-10 Minutes)

Appendix A: Requests of the Christ Child

- Ask God to speak to you during this devotional time.
- Pray for the Christmas season.

- - Pray for Christmas worship services and celebrations in the community.
  - Pray for your church and your Christmas celebrations.
  - Pray for our Nation during this holiday period.
- In Appendix A, write any specific Christmas concerns that need continued prayers.
- Pray for needs.
  - Pray specifically for the people in your lives.
  - Pray for your church.
  - Tell God your concerns and needs.
- In Appendix A, write any other specific requests that need continued prayers.
- Ask for knowledge of His will for you this Christmas and the power to carry it out.
- Ask the Holy Spirit to interpret the scriptures you are about to read.

Appendix B: Gifts from the Christ Child

- Think about your blessings this Christmas.
- Praise God for His blessings.
- In Appendix B, write your top three blessings.

Appendix C: Gifts to the Christ Child

- Ask God to help develop the attitude that each gift given to anyone is a gift to the Christ Child.
- Ask Jesus what He wants for Christmas this year.
- In Appendix C, prayerfully, fill in any gifts you plan to purchase between now and Christmas. Fill in as much information as you currently have.

Appendix D: Celebrations for the Christ Child

- Pray about all of the Christmas celebrations on your calendar. This includes all family, church, community, and other Christmas events which you plan to attend, host, or participate.
- Turn to Appendix D and list these Christmas celebrations, praying about each one.
- Fill in your "To Do" list, praying about each action.

Bible Study (10-15 Minutes)

Christmas is a time for fellowship with God, families, friends, and our church. God tells us, "It is not good for you to be alone" (Genesis 2:18). Healthy loving hearts need fellowship. If we fellowship with God and open our eyes and look around, God will send us people with whom to have deep and intimate fellowship. His word teaches us about godly fellowship.

Background scripture

The background Scripture is Luke 1:1-56. Open your Bible to the familiar passage. Today's devotion studies the fellowship between the two godly women God chose to begin the very first Christmas. We will study how Mary and Elizabeth fellowshipped with God and each other. We will study the following aspects of their fellowship: Love, the Holy Spirit, God the Father, and Jesus Christ.

God chose two unlikely women for His model for fellowship: Elizabeth who was too old to have a child and Mary who was too young and innocent. They were both a "disgrace" by their world's standards. Elizabeth's disgrace was her barrenness and Mary's, a pregnancy out of wedlock.

Our Holy God loves to do the unexpected. The world judged them unworthy but God judged Mary and Elizabeth worthy above other women. He chose Elizabeth to bear the son that would tell the world about the Christ Child. He chose Mary to bear His son.

Background - Elizabeth

Read Luke 1:5-7. Elizabeth had been married for many years to Zechariah. Both Zechariah and Elizabeth were descendents of priests. They lived blameless lives. Zechariah was faithful to his priestly calling. Their religion taught them that children were blessings from God and in that time, people assumed the inability to have children was a sign of God's punishment. Most likely, Elizabeth and Zechariah were the subject of gossip and/or questions. How do you think Elizabeth felt about being barren?

_____

_____

Read Luke 1:25. Elizabeth desperately wanted children. She pleaded with God and had faith He would answer. She waited and probably held her breath each month, feeling the shame and disgrace of her barrenness as the years progressed. Miraculously, God finally answered her prayers. How does she feel now?

_____

_____

Read Luke 1:16-17. God planned Elizabeth's blessing for years (maybe since the beginning of creation) and gave even more than she asked for. What was the special purpose of Elizabeth's child?

_____

_____

Background - Mary

Mary was a young woman with the same dreams other young women had. Her questions to the angel indicate she was intelligent, confident, honorable, and pure. Mary was engaged to a kind Jewish man named Joseph and she expected to follow in the footsteps of the faithful people who taught her how to live and love.

Read Luke 1:29-31 and Luke 1:12-13. Again, God does the unexpected. An angel named Gabriel appeared to her, changing Mary's plans. Gabriel had been busy, visiting Zechariah and announcing Elizabeth's pregnancy. Understandably, Gabriel frightened both Zechariah and Mary. We can only hope Gabriel did not take these reactions personally. In fact, he must be used to these reactions because he had his response ready.

Read Luke 1:34. Gabriel told Mary she was going to bear the Son of God. Mary's parents had obviously told her the "facts of life" because she knew pregnancy was impossible. Why was Mary confused?

_____

_____

Read Luke 1:38. In the end, Mary humbly accepted the will of God. She even rejoiced in the news. What was her answer?

_____

_____

We can imagine the conversation with Mary's mother. "An angel said what?" Mary must have been tempted to ask Gabriel to come back and explain this to her mother. We do know that Mary left her home in a hurry (Luke 1:39). Did you ever wonder if her mother wanted to whisk her away before the pregnancy showed?

Love at Christmas

Read Luke 1:43-44. Mary went straight to Elizabeth's house. Here we have one of the most beautiful demonstrations of love and friendship recorded in the Bible as these women shared their faith and joy, quoting Scripture, and worshiping God as they talked. What did Elizabeth say to Mary?

_____

_____

Baby John joined the celebration. What did he do?

_____

_____

God, the Holy Spirit

Read Luke 1:41-42. How do we know the Holy Spirit was part of their fellowship?

_____

_____

God, the Father

Read Luke 1:46-47. True fellowship includes worship of the Holy Father. Mary and Elizabeth praised God together as they sang and quoted scriptures. Write the words of their worship and let your spirit rejoice in God your savior.

_____

_____

God, the Son

Read Luke 1:42. The final piece of true fellowship is Jesus Christ. What were Elizabeth's words to Mary?

_____

_____

Application (5-10 Minutes)

Making It Personal

List the people with whom you will fellowship the most this Christmas.

_____

_____

Whom do you love?

_____

_____

With whom do you share godly fellowship? Which relationships include the presence of God the Father, Son, and Holy Spirit?

_____

_____

Which relationships need improvement?

_____

_____

Ask God to help you improve your relationships. What can you do to improve your relationships this Christmas?

_____

_____

If you are lonely and need more fellowship, write a letter asking God to meet your needs. Specifically, ask God to send you one new person today.

_____

_____

Praying Continuously (1 Thessalonians 5:17)

- At meals and bedtime, pray for those closest to you.
- Tell at least one friend or family member how important they are to you.
- Look for His answers throughout the day.

Ending The Day

- Ask God to help you with your fellowship with Him and those closest to you.
- How was your fellowship on this first day of the Christmas season?
- Confess your failures and claim your victories.

The Eyes of the Christ Child

Meditation (3-5 Minutes)

Begin by being still before God. Meditate on the words "For unto us a child is born, unto us a son is given: and the government shall be upon his shoulder: and his name shall be called Wonderful, Counselor, The mighty God, The everlasting Father, The Prince of Peace." (Isaiah 9:6 KJV)

- Be still and know He is God.
- Think about Jesus as a child. What can you imagine Him doing? Do you think He enjoyed getting and receiving gifts? Imagine how the Christ Child would experience modern-day Christmas. View this Christmas through the eyes of the Christ Child.
- Let Him be your Wonderful Counselor. Surrender your problems and seek His wisdom.
- Let Him be your Mighty God. Surrender to His power. Feel and claim His power.
- Let Him be your Everlasting Father. Bask in His love as you feel His arms around you.
- Let Him be your Prince of Peace. Release all contentious thoughts or worries and experience His peace.
- Listen to the voice of God.

Prayer (5-10 Minutes)

Appendix A: Requests of the Christ Child

- Ask God to speak to you during this devotional time.
- Pray specifically for those who need to experience Christmas through the eyes of Christ.

- In Appendix A, specifically name those in emotional or physical pain.
- In Appendix A, specifically name the non-Christians in your life.
- Prayerfully update Appendix A with new requests and any answers from God.
- Praise God for His answers.
- Ask for knowledge of His will for you this Christmas and the power to carry it out.
- Ask the Holy Spirit to interpret the scriptures you are about to read.

Appendix B: Gifts from the Christ Child

- Praise God for His blessings.
- Add three more blessings to Appendix B.

Appendix C: Gifts to the Christ Child

- Ask God to give you His spirit as you buy gifts for others.
- Turn to Appendix C and update the list.

Appendix D: Celebrations for the Christ Child

- Turn to Appendix D and update your "To Do" list.
- Ask God if there are other celebrations in which you should participate. List them in Appendix D.

Bible Study

Jesus came to earth like any other red-faced screaming baby. People celebrated His birth and gave gifts. He had to learn to walk, talk, and dress himself. He grew up loved by His earthly mother and father. He may have even had pimples, chicken pox, and the measles. As a child, Jesus taught adults and as an adult, He instructed us to let children be our teachers.

Background Scripture

Read Matthew 9:13-15, Mark 10:13-16, and Luke 18:15-17 and notice how Jesus took time to be with children. How did He treat these children? What did He do for them?

_____

_____

What lesson was Jesus trying to teach His pious and impatient disciples and us?

_____

_____

The Faith of a Child

Wide-eyed, brown-haired, giggly, wiggly Lauren was eight years old. "I can't wait for Christmas. It's my first Christmas as a Christian." Earlier that year, Lauren asked Jesus to be a part of her life. "I was baptized," she told me excitedly.

Lauren lived in a godly home and attended church all of her life. Jesus had always been part of her life in some way. I questioned her further. "You already knew about Jesus. Why is this Christmas different?"

"Christmas has to be different because everything is different now. Jesus is my friend. I need Him this year because two of my other friends moved away. Jesus will never move away."

"What do you do with Jesus?" I asked.

"I talk to him. My brother is sick so I asked God to help him. My Daddy needs a job. I told Jesus."

"What is your favorite part of Christmas?" I asked.

"Church is fun at Christmas. I love singing the Christmas carols. I get to go up front and light a candle." I asked about her favorite Christmas service. "Christmas Eve. We turn off the lights and light candles."

"What about the Bible? Do you have a favorite verse?" I prompted.

Without hesitation, she proudly answered, "Genesis 1:1. I can say it. 'In the beginning, God created the heavens and the earth.' This was the first verse I memorized. It reminds me that God made me. My favorite verse in the New Testament is John 3:16. 'For God so loved the world, that He gave His only begotten Son, that whosoever believeth in him should not perish, but have everlasting life.'"

"Lauren," I smiled. "What does that mean to you?"

"This tells me I will live forever with Jesus." Out of the mouths of babes.

Read John 3:16 and Genesis 1:1. What do these scriptures mean to you?

_____

_____

Since Lauren is just eight, I knew there had to be more to Christmas for her. "What about gifts?" I quizzed. "What was the favorite gift you ever got?"

Her face lit up. "I love gifts. When I was three, I got a toy car that fit over my legs. I sat on the ground and pretended to drive. It had a steering wheel and a gearshift. Driving this car made me feel like a grown up. When I got older, I liked different stuff. I gave the toy car to a girl in my church. Now I like Barbie Christmas gifts. Wearing a Barbie nightgown makes me feel pretty. I want a new Barbie for Christmas."

"Lauren, why do you think we celebrate Christmas?" I was expecting her to say that we celebrate the birth of Jesus. Her answer was better.

"We celebrate God's gift to us. Christmas reminds me of a song I sing in church. This song says we do not have to go looking for the gift of Christmas. Jesus is the gift that comes to us."

In what way does Lauren have the eyes of the Christ Child?

_____

_____

Read Luke 18:17. How are we to receive the kingdom of God?

_____

_____

A footnote to Lauren's story is that her brother got well and her father found a job.

Application (5-10 Minutes)

Making It Personal

Name and pray for your favorite Christmas celebration. Why do you like it so much?

_____

_____

Write your favorite Bible verse.

_____

_____

What was your favorite Christmas gift? Thank God for it.

_____

_____

Name a child who is innocent, bright, and full of joy. This can be an adult that you remember as a child or a child you currently know.

_____

How would this child react to life in your current circumstances this Christmas?

_____

_____

What areas of your life need the eyes of the Christ Child?

_____

_____

Ask God to help you have a childlike spirit throughout the day.

Praying Continuously (1 Thessalonians 5:17)

Stop and briefly pray when you feel strong emotions (i.e., impatience, anger, excitement, frustration, or joy). As you feel each of these emotions, ask yourself this question: "If I were experiencing this with the faith of a child, how would I be reacting?" Continually pray for the faith of a child.

Ending the Day

- Thank God for the children in your life.
- Did you have the eyes of the Christ Child today?
- Confess if necessary.
- Ask God for the eyes of the Christ Child.

Giving Gifts on Purpose

Meditation (3-5 Minutes)

Begin by being still before God. Meditate on the words "A gift opens the way for the giver and ushers him into the presence of the great." (Proverbs 18:16 NIV)

- Be still and know He is God.
- Think about some of the Christmas gifts you have given in years past.
    - Were they from the heart?
    - How did you pick them out?
    - Did you pray about them?
    - Did you enjoy giving them?
    - Did they serve a purpose in God's kingdom?
- Picture yourself standing at a door on Christmas morning. You have trouble knocking because your arms are overflowing with gifts. Excited children quickly open the door. What is the look in their eyes as they see your gifts?
- Picture yourself standing at the door of the "Presence of the Great." You have trouble knocking because your arms are overflowing with gifts. "The Great" quickly opens the door. What is the look in His eyes as He sees your gifts?
- Sit quietly and experience the "Presence of the Great."
- Listen to the voice of God.

Prayer (5-10 Minutes)

Appendix A: Requests of the Christ Child

- Ask God to speak to you during this devotional time.
- Ask God to help you understand the purpose of giving gifts at Christmas.
- Ask God to help you release:
  - Resentments of family pressure to give more.
  - Fear that the gifts you can afford will not be enough.
  - Worry about the time it takes to buy or make gifts.
  - Stinginess or greed.
- Turn to Appendix A: pray and update.
- Ask for knowledge of His will for you this Christmas and the power to carry it out.
- Ask the Holy Spirit to interpret the scriptures you are about to read.

Appendix B: Gifts from the Christ Child

- In Appendix B, list your favorite Christmas gift.

Appendix C: Gifts to the Christ Child

- Ask God to guide you as you pick out your Christmas gifts.
- Thank God that these gifts will usher you into the "Presence of the Great."
- Scan Appendix C, thinking of these gifts as gifts to the Christ Child.
  - Ask the Christ Child what He wants for Christmas.
  - Update the list and make any changes you are inspired to make.

Appendix D: Celebrations for the Christ Child

- Turn to Appendix D and notice which activities will usher you into the "Presence of the Great."
- Update your "To Do" list.

Bible Study (10-15 Minutes)

God gave the first Christmas gift, which each person chooses to accept or reject. Those that accept the gift celebrate Christmas because God sent His Son for us.

Most of us give gifts at Christmas. Merchants plan much of their economic year based on expectations for Christmas. Studies show that each American spends an average of $800 a year for Christmas. Since many people in America spend nothing for Christmas, that means many spend more than $800. Is Christmas too commercialized? Do we spend too much time and money on Christmas? Do the gifts we give get in the way of the meaning of Christmas? Write how you feel about the commercialization of Christmas.

_____

_____

The answers to the above questions lie in the purpose of the gifts we give. Giving gifts "on purpose" can be a joy. Giving gifts to God's children can be part of our relationship with God. Like everything else in our relationship with God, gift giving at Christmas can serve God's purpose in the lives of the giver and receiver.

Background Scripture

Read Matthew 25:40. When we give gifts, to whom are we really giving? _____
Read Matthew 2:1-11. The first Christmas gifts given to the Christ Child were from Wise Men from the East. Note the time and effort that the men went to in order to celebrate this first Christmas. What obstacles did they have to overcome?

_____

_____

These Wise Men were both generous and frugal. We know the gifts were precious to them because we see the words "they opened their treasures." We also know they could afford to give what they gave because of the word "their." These men did not "Master Charge" their gifts to the Christ Child. What gifts did the Wise Men give to the Christ Child?

_____

What did the Wise Men do as they gave these gifts?

_____

Jesus was a baby and had no personal use for gold. Like us, the Wise Men gave their gifts to Jesus through other people. Who do you think really used the gifts from the Wise Men?

_____

What purpose do you think these gifts served?

_____

_____

Were the gifts too commercial? Did the Wise Men spend too much? Did these gifts get in the way of the true meaning of Christmas?

Gifts with the Purpose of Love

Read Jesus' command in Mark 12:30-31. What are the five ways we are to love God?

At Christmas, we demonstrate our love for God by giving gifts. Give an example of a gift that can help others fulfill Jesus' greatest commandment to love.

<u>Loving God With Our Hearts: Felltowship Gifts</u>

We love God with our hearts when we fellowship with Him and others. Many and possibly most Christmas gifts are for fellowship. Our fellowship includes playing and visiting together. Most people remember the toys they get at Christmas. Gifts of fellowship are anything we enjoy doing with other people, anything that communicates love. Fellowship gifts can include games, toys, or even the redecorating of a family room. We can love the Lord God with our heart when we play with the abandonment of a child. Name a potential gift of fellowship you have given.

<u>Loving God With Our Souls: Worship Gifts</u>

Our souls worship God. We love God with our souls as we praise Him, pray, and spend daily time with Him. If we love God, our souls will worship Him for all eternity. Many gifts can assist with worship. An example of a worship gift could be Christian music and even a stereo to play it on. Yes, that stereo may play other types of music, but its purpose would be to worship God. Name a potential gift of worship you have given.

Loving God With Our Mind: Discipleship Gifts

We love the Lord God with our mind when we strengthen our mind or learn more about God. As we study, we become disciples of Christ. We educate our minds so we can fulfill our earthly callings. Discipleship gifts help the recipient strengthen his or her mind. These gifts can include anything that makes us better people. Educational toys and books, Bible study books, or journals can be examples of discipleship gifts. Name a potential gift of discipleship you have given.

_____

Loving God With Our Strength: Ministry Gifts

We love God with our strength when we minister to other people. Ministry gifts are practical gifts that make someone's life more functional. Examples can be appliances, tools, socks, and even the dreaded tie. We love the Lord God with our strength when we have the tools we need to take care of the housekeeping items that God assigns. Name a potential gift of ministry you have given.

_____

Loving Our Neighbors As Ourselves: Mission Gifts

We love our neighbor as ourselves when we help our neighbors find God. At Christmas, many people donate to missions or help with mission projects. An example of a personal gift of missions could be giving a Bible to a non-Christian or feeding the homeless. Name a potential gift of mission you have given.

_____

As we give gifts this year, let us give them purposefully. As we receive gifts on behalf of the Christ Child, let us use them for His purpose. For the next five days, we will read stories of people that found purpose in the gifts they gave and received. We will learn to apply God's greatest commandments to our Christmas gift giving, loving God with our entire heart, soul, mind, and strength and loving our neighbors as ourselves. Together, we will worship God as we learn how to give gifts to the Christ Child.

Application (5-10 Minutes)

Making It Personal

What is your attitude about giving gifts? Are you thinking of gifts you give to others as gifts to the Christ Child? Do you resent gift giving? Do you delight in giving gifts or find yourself making speeches about "commercialism" or "the selfish demands of gift giving?" How can you improve your attitude?

_____

_____

Like the Wise Men, do you bow down and worship Jesus as you present Him with His gifts? How can you better worship as you buy and give gifts?

_____

_____

"Opening our treasures" can include giving gifts, money, precious items, or time. How are you "opening your treasures" this year?

_____

_____

Each of us has a different amount in our "treasury." Can you afford the gifts you are giving?

_____

_____

Praying Continuously (1 Thessalonians 5:17)

Throughout your day, try to remember the meaningful Christmas gifts you have received. Think about their practical uses, how they helped you love God or your neighbor. Praise God for the gifts.

Every time you see Christmas lights, thank God for the privilege of being able to give gifts at Christmas.

Ending The Day

- Thank God. Thank Him for His Christmas gift to us, for the model set by the Wise Men, and for the privilege of giving gifts to others in His name.
- Confess. If you are resentful or feeling trapped into giving gifts at Christmas, confess. Ask God for help with your attitude. If you have not been "opening your treasures" or you have been spending too much, confess. If you have not been taking delight or worshiping as you give Him His gifts, confess.

Ministry Gifts

Meditation (3-5 Minutes)

Begin by being still before God. Meditate on the words "He is before all things, and in Him all things hold together." (Colossians 1:17 NIV)

- Be still and know He is God.
- Think about your life. What is causing you stress? For what are you grateful?
- Meditate on the words, "He is before all things."
    - Your father knows everything you are going through.
    - He was there before you, preparing the way.
    - Do you believe that God was "before you" during your difficulties?
    - Take a moment to bask in the relief of God's promise to be "before all things."
- Think about the words, "In Him all things hold together."
    - Are you in Him?
    - If so, everything in your life will hold together and improve your personal ministry.
    - Think about a difficult time and how it made you stronger.
    - Bask in the relief that "all things will hold together."
- Listen to the voice of God.

Prayer (5-10 Minutes)

Appendix A: Requests of the Christ Child

- Ask God to speak to you during this devotional time.
- Ask God for understanding:
    - Of how your life is holding together.
    - Of what is happening around you.
- Ask for wisdom:
    - To know how to respond to your circumstances.
    - To be able to fulfill your personal ministry this Christmas.
- List any new requests in Appendix A. Pray and update.
- Ask for knowledge of His will for you this Christmas and the power to carry it out.
- Ask the Holy Spirit to interpret the scriptures you are about to read.

Appendix B: Gifts from the Christ Child

- Think about the practical Christmas gifts you have received. Examples might be a blender, toaster, or a set of tools. How did they help you fulfill your personal ministries or calling?
- Praise God for the practical gifts He gives you.
- Turn to Appendix B and list a practical gift that was a blessing.

Appendix C: Gifts to the Christ Child

- Turn to Appendix C, pray and update.
- Do you plan to give any practical gifts this year?
- How will they help the recipients?
- Pray that these gifts will serve God's purpose.

Appendix D: Celebrations for the Christ Child

- Are you taking a disciplined approach to planning your celebrations?
- Turn to Appendix D and update your "To Do" list, praying about each action.
    - Ask God what practical things you need to do to serve others this Christmas. Add them to your "To Do" list.
    - Ask God if there is anything unnecessary on this list.
    - Cross out unnecessary actions or celebrations.

Bible Study (10-15 Minutes)

God formed us to serve Him. He carefully chooses our service to Him. Occasionally, God calls us to do dramatic or great things but more often, our calling is to perform every day tasks for the Glory of God. Our service may seem insignificant until we understand how "all things hold together."

God expects us to wake up every morning asking for knowledge of His will for that day and the power to carry it out. If asked, God will grant this knowledge and give us the power to fulfill our purpose. If we are pursuing our purpose, God ordains each of our daily tasks. These tasks will hold together and form a tapestry that mysteriously and wondrously ministers to the world around us. We minister as we live our lives, loving God with our strength.

Background Scripture

Read Colossians 1:9-12. We are to ask God to fill us with the knowledge of His will through all _____.

We pray for knowledge of His will so we can live a life worthy of the Lord and please Him in every way. Through the ordinary tasks of our lives, we bear fruit and grow in:

_____

_____

Our strength comes from God as He blesses us with "all power according to His glorious might." What comes from this strength? _____ and _____.

Read Jesus' prayer in John 17:1-5. Jesus' work on earth was complete. Write His prayer in verse 4.

_____

_____

Today, how are you working toward completing the work given to you?

_____

_____

Write Jesus' prayer in verse 5 and ask that He glorify you in His presence.

_____

_____

23

Many gifts we give and receive at Christmas facilitate our ability to complete God's assignments. God goes before us in all things and plans what we need. Our gifts "hold together" and enable us to fulfill our ministries. Like Jesus, we love God with our strength as we glorify Him by completing the work He gave us to do.

Ministry Gift: Fountain Pen

My daddy, Cecil, grew up in a home with seven children. The family didn't have much money but on Christmas morning, each child got a stocking, containing all of his or her Christmas gifts. Each stocking had an apple, orange, and some pressed Christmas candy. "Our mouth watered for that candy as we tried to fall asleep on Christmas Eve," Daddy reported. "We were allowed to pick one twenty-five cent and one ten cent toy to go in our stockings."

"Did you have a favorite gift?" I asked.

"I always asked for a fountain pen. You could get a wonderful fountain pen and pencil set for twenty-five cents. I used my pen all year in school. I even loaned it out to help my brothers and sisters."

While pens are essential to our everyday lives, many of us take them for granted. There are always plenty to use. Most can find several at the bottom of old and discarded purses or briefcases. If we forget one, we ask someone to lend us one. We casually leave them on counters or walk off with ones that belong to others. Most people won't return just to retrieve a lost twenty-five cent pen.

Would we be so careless with our pens if we could only have one per year? I have a vision of a young Cecil, 70 years ago, feeling blessed to have his very own fountain pen. He treasured and cared for that fountain pen. "Did you ever lose it?" I asked.

"No," Daddy answered. "I took it with me everywhere."

However, little Cecil was not completely practical. He also had a playful side. "For my ten-cent gift, I always asked for a toy. My favorite was a toy monkey that climbed a stick."

Ministry Gift: Shoeboxes Filled With Soap

Our church has a ministry for migrant workers and their children. Many fill shoeboxes with gifts for the children. The gifts the children appreciate most are the ones that are the most practical. They love soaps, toothpaste, toothbrushes, and deodorants.

Most people in America take practical items for granted. We travel and stay at hotels. We casually open a bar of soap or bottle of shampoo and use only part of the contents. The migrant children open these shoebox treasures and joyfully use all of the contents. When a bottle of shampoo is empty, they probably fill it with water to take full advantage of the contents.

Like little Cecil these children are not completely practical, either. They giggle and glow as they play with the toys in the shoeboxes.

Ministry Gift: China

My mama, Grace, has always loved Christmas. She grew up in a Christian home that made a big deal about Christmas. One gift that stood out to her was a set of dishes. This gift cost her parents nothing but time and effort. Mama married just after World War II. Traditionally, people give china at weddings but because of the war, stores could not get china. Instead, they sold redeemable certificates for later. Mama received china certificates at most of her wedding showers.

"The store called my parents when the china arrived," said Mama. "Instead of calling me, Mama and Daddy went to the store and redeemed all of the certificates. They wrapped the china and put it under the tree. I was thrilled on Christmas morning when I opened my china." Newly married Grace, received this china twice, once at her wedding showers and once at Christmas. "I loved it both times."

Mama's parents ministered to her by doing an errand that would have taken her time. They ministered to her spirit by surprising her and making her feel treasured. Mama ministers to others by using the china to serve people in her home.

Mama is also not completely practical. She loves getting gold jewelry for Christmas.

Ministry Gift: A Warning

There is a word of caution about giving practical ministry gifts. Not everyone appreciates them. Ministry gifts are for the practical or those in need. Ministry gifts may include things like blenders, vacuum cleaners, irons, and mops. One woman complained, "My family only gives these gifts so I can do more work."

If you are very practical, you may tend to give practical gifts yourself. Gifts are for the Christ Child and not for us and should model the receiver's preferences. The Christ Child came to meet the needs and even the wants of His children. Make sure you are following His model as you give your gifts.

Read Hebrews 13:20-21. If we ask, God will equip us with what we need to fulfill the ministries of our lives. At Christmas, we have the opportunity to give gifts that help people fulfill their personal ministries.

Application (5-10 Minutes)

Making It Personal

How do you love God with your strength this Christmas? How are you ministering to the people around you in the ordinary tasks of your day?

_____

_____

List any gifts you could ask family members for that would assist with your ministry.

_____

_____

Pray for the ministries of people around you. Ask God to show you ways to make their lives and ministries easier and more effective.

Praying Continuously (1 Thessalonians 5:17)

As you go through your day, look for people helping others. Be sure to notice the simplest things. Notice the tools they use to help other people.

- Praise God for the people and the tools you observe.
- Ask God to send you three ways to help other people today.
- Take the opportunities God hands you. These opportunities may be simple or complicated.
- Communicate your ministry gift needs listed in the section above to a family member or a friend.

Ending The Day

- Did you carry out your daily tasks to the glory of God?
- Did you minister to those around you? If not, confess.
- Thank God for the ministers in your life.
- Ask God to provide the tools you need to fulfill your ministry this Christmas.
- Praise God for the tools He sends you.

Fellowship Gifts

Meditation (3-5 Minutes)

Begin by being still before God. Meditate on the words "Thou art worthy, O Lord, to receive glory and honor and power: for thou hast created all things, and for thy pleasure they are and were created." (Revelation 4:11 KJV)

- Be still and know He is God.
- Meditate on God's worthiness.
- Think about His glory, honor, and power.
    - Imagine His glory.
    - Give Him honor.
    - Feel His power.
- Meditate on His creations.
    - Picture the most beautiful places you have seen.
    - Think about the people you know.
    - Think about His wonders on earth.
- Enjoy being God's pleasure.
- Listen to the voice of God.

Prayer (5-10 Minutes)

Appendix A: Requests of the Christ Child

- Ask God to speak to you during this devotional time.
- Think about the people with whom you fellowship.

- - Pray for their needs and list them in Appendix A.
  - Ask God to help you learn to have better fellowship with the people in your life.
- Think about your church.
  - Pray for her needs and list them in Appendix A.
  - Ask God to help you learn to have better fellowship through your church.
- Think about your relationship with the Christ Child.
  - In Appendix A, Ask God to help you learn to have better fellowship with Jesus.
- Update Appendix A with any answered prayers.
- Ask for knowledge of His will for you this Christmas and the power to carry it out.
- Ask the Holy Spirit to interpret the scriptures you are about to read.

Appendix B: Gifts from the Christ Child

- Praise God for fellowship with Him, your church, and the people in your life.
- In Appendix B, list specific fellowship blessings.

Appendix C: Gifts to the Christ Child

- God longs for fellowship with you this Christmas. He created you for His pleasure and delights in you. Offer Him yourself for Christmas.
- Turn to Appendix C. Will your list delight your recipients? Pray and update the list.

Appendix D: Celebrations for the Christ Child

- Turn to Appendix D. Note the events that are for fellowship.
- Update your "To Do" list, praying about each action.

Bible Study (10-15 Minutes)

One way to love God with our heart is to fellowship with God, friends, family, and our church. God created us for His pleasure. The word pleasure means a source of enjoyment or delight. When we fellowship with God He takes delight in us and wants to give us the delights of our hearts. He is delighted when we delight each other. Gifts of fellowship delight God and others and fill our pockets with love and fun.

Background Scripture

Read Psalm 149:4. Say the words, "The Lord takes delight in me." Write and memorize them.

_____

_____

Read Zephaniah 3:17. Write out the first phrase, changing the words "your" and "you" to "my" and "me."

_____

_____

God is mighty enough to save us from anything, including the Christmas rush. This Christmas, He is taking delight in us. Harried as Christmas is, if we let Him, He will quiet us. What will He use to quiet us?

_____

_____

We sing Carols at Christmas. We rejoice over the birth of the Christ Child. God is also rejoicing over us. While we are singing, how is He rejoicing over us?

_____

_____

Read Ephesians 1:4-5. God sent His son Jesus to earth for us. What were we predestined to be?

_____

Why did He do this for us? _____

God took great pleasure in giving us our very first Christmas gift. Is it any wonder that so many of the Christmas gifts we give each other are for the purpose of pleasure?

Read 1 John 3:1. How great is our Father's love? What are we?

_____

_____

_____

29

Fellowship Gift: A Charm Bracelet

Nancy grew up in a practical home where only practical Christmas gifts were expected. There never seemed to be enough money. At Christmas, she asked for many things and didn't get most of them. "Once, I wanted a Fish Basket purse that cost $10. I begged my parents for one. I offered to work and help pay for it. My father refused and said I had no idea how much $10 really was. For them, $10 was a fortune.

One Christmas, I asked for a silver charm bracelet. I felt guilty for asking but I longed for this bracelet. It was expensive and had no practical purpose. After the Fish Basket incident, I didn't expect to receive this charm bracelet."

When Nancy opened her Christmas gift, she was shocked and delighted to find a silver charm bracelet. "I will remember this gift forever." Forty years later, she still remembers the delight of this gift. "My parents had sacrificed to get this gift. I felt loved every time I wore the bracelet."

Fellowship Gift: The Puppy

Duncan was four. "I remember lying in bed and hearing a puppy crying. I got up in the middle of the night and found my new Christmas puppy. I loved it and played with it until way into the night. Suddenly, I became aware of how many other presents were under the tree. I decided I wanted to know what was in the packages."

While his parents were peacefully sleeping, he proceeded to open every single package that was under the tree. His parents woke the next morning and had to re-wrap everyone's Christmas presents. The Christmas he remembers most fondly includes the pleasure of the fellowship with his puppy and the spanking he got from his father.

Fellowship Gift: The Ski Trip

Josh and Jeremy are my nephews. Their favorite Christmas gift was a snow skiing trip to Colorado we took as an extended family. Nine members of our family decided to give each other the gift of fellowship and to spend a week together in a condo. "We had a wonderful time," Josh reported. "We spent our days on the slopes and our evenings playing games, sitting around a fire, and drinking hot chocolate."

Fellowship Gift: A Gold Chain

My husband, Bob, says one of his favorite presents is the gold chain he wears every day. "I have no idea how many years ago you gave it to me." He seldom takes it off. "Wearing it reminds me of our love. It also reminds me to pray for you." My husband is a smart man. As I select his Christmas gift, his affirmations puts me in a mood to be more generous.

Fellowship Gifts: A Warning

There are certainly temptations when giving and receiving gifts of the heart. Some people enjoy gifts of fellowship so much that they miss the pleasure of all the other purposes in giving. Some may be so practical that they fail to enjoy a gift that is purely for fellowship or pleasure.

If you are one who loves gifts of the heart, you may be tempted to give no other kind of gift. Gift giving is not for us. We are to look at the needs and the desires of the people receiving our gifts on behalf of the Christ Child. The Christ Child wants them delighted. People may have specific practical needs during the Christmas season. If someone is practical, a fellowship gift may seem too frivolous.

Application (5-10 Minutes)

Making It Personal

God takes pleasure in us. Do you take pleasure in Him? How can you improve?

_____

_____

Do you take pleasure in your family? How can you improve?

_____

_____

Do you take pleasure in your church? How can you improve?

_____

_____

Take an inventory:

- Do the lights and the trees make you grin?_____
- Do you get excited about the gifts you are given? _____
- Do your gifts delight the people around you? _____
- Are you delighted with this Christmas season? If not, what would it take to delight you?

_____

_____

What fellowship gift would delight you?

_____

_____

Praying Continuously (1 Thessalonians 5:17)

- Think like a child. Children understand that living life for sheer delight is acceptable. As you go through your day, look for ways to be delighted.
- As you perform each daily task, ask yourself:
  - Do I take pleasure in this task? If the answer is yes, praise God for the task.
  - If the answer is no, ask God to help you take delight in the task.
- At least once during the day, take a moment and give the gift of your time for the sake of fellowship.
- At least once during the day, do something for yourself that has no other purpose than your pleasure. Blow bubbles. Buy yourself a small gift. Read the comic strips. Take a bubble bath. Step outside and enjoy the wind blowing on your face.
- At each mealtime and at bedtime, take a moment to find delight in God's presence (or is it His presents?).

Ending The Day

- Thank God for fellowship at Christmas. Thank Him for taking delight in us.
- Tell God how much you love Him.
- If you do not take delight in Christmas, confess and ask God to give you the heart of a child.
- If your gifts do not delight God and people, ask God to teach you how to demonstrate His delight in us through the gifts you give to others. If you do not know how to relax and enjoy the fellowship of giving and receiving gifts, ask God to help you.

Discipleship Gifts

Meditation (3-5 Minutes)

Begin by being still before God. Meditate on the words "Then Jesus said to His disciples, 'If anyone desires to be my disciple, let him deny himself [disregard, lose sight of, and forget himself and his own interests] and take up his cross and follow Me [cleave steadfastly to Me, conform wholly to My example in living and, if need be, in dying, also]. For whoever is bent on saving his [temporal] life [his comfort and security here] shall lose it [eternal life]; and whoever loses his life [his comfort and security here] for My sake shall find it [life everlasting]'." (Matthew 16:24-25 The Amplified Bible)

- Be still and know He is God.
- Do you desire to be Jesus' disciple?
- Are you willing:
    - To deny yourself (forget yourself and your own interests)?
    - To lose your life for the sake of finding it?
- Are you willing to take Christ's cross and:
    - Cleave steadfastly to Him?
    - Conform wholly to His example in living and, if need be, dying?
- Are you willing to lose your comfort and security for the sake of being a disciple of Christ?
- Be honest before God.
- Accept His grace in your honesty.
- Let His spirit speak to you.
- Listen to the voice of God.

Prayer (5-10 Minutes)

Appendix A: Requests of the Christ Child

- Ask God to speak to you during this devotional time.
- Ask God to help you be willing to be a disciple of Christ.
- If you are holding on to anything temporal, turn to Appendix A and ask God to remove your unnecessary "need."
- Prayerfully update Appendix A with new requests and any answers from God.
- Ask for knowledge of His will for you this Christmas and the power to carry it out.
- Ask the Holy Spirit to interpret the scriptures you are about to read.

Appendix B: Gifts from the Christ Child

- Think about gifts that have helped you be a better disciple. As they come to mind:
  - Praise God for them.
  - List them in Appendix B.
- If nothing comes to mind, ask God to send you a gift this Christmas that will help you be a better disciple.

Appendix C: Gifts to the Christ Child

- Turn to Appendix C: Pray and update.
- Do any of your gifts help people to become better disciples?
- Ask God if you need to make any adjustments.

Appendix D: Celebrations for the Christ Child

- Turn to Appendix D. Do any of your planned Christmas celebrations help you become a better disciple of Christ?
- Update your "To Do" list, praying about each action.

Bible Study (10-15 Minutes)

One of our purposes on earth is to become a disciple of Jesus. We love the Lord with our entire mind when we educate that mind to become a better person. Gifts that help us be better disciples are discipleship gifts.

Instructions for following Jesus start when we are young. Jesus had a pocket full of knowledge and was a good student. When He was twelve, His knowledge of the law astounded the teachers in the temple. Joseph most likely trained Jesus to be a carpenter, a trade Jesus practiced until He began His ministry. Disciples of Jesus were from Jewish families who made sure they were well versed in Jewish law and properly trained for their various trades. Whether it's formal or informal, being properly educated for our call needs a combination of spiritual and secular training.

Background Scripture

Read Luke 2:46-48. Think about Jesus as a boy. Describe Him. Describe His ability to study and learn. Describe His intelligence and curiosity. Was He a good student? How long was His attention span?

_____

_____

Read 2 Chronicles 34:10-12. What types of careers do you see in this Scripture? Do you know people who perform these today?

_____

_____

Note that the managers handled payroll and paid the workers for their labor. How did the workers perform?

_____

Think about these workers. What training do you think they had?

_____

_____

Read 2 Timothy 2:15. Whose approval are we seeking when we study?

_____

How should we perform our jobs?

_____

Read Matthew 28:19. What does Jesus tell us to do?

_____

_____

Gifts that help make disciples are wonderful Christmas gifts. Christmas is a perfect opportunity to make disciples of children. Children have the opportunity to pray about the gifts they give, help with mission projects, and give to others in need. Guiding them through this process will help them throughout their lives.

Discipleship Gift: Bible Software

Many study aids assist us with our Christian discipleship. A few years ago, my husband gave me Bible software, which I use almost every day. By typing in one word, I can find various scriptures on a topic. I can look at multiple translations and even study Greek and Hebrew. I used the Bible software to find the scriptures for this devotion.

The next Christmas, my mother asked for Bible software. Now both of us are able to search the entire Bible and conduct research on any subject. In a matter of seconds, we can find all of the places God says, "I love you."

Discipleship Gift: Devotional and Other Christian Books

I enjoy reading Oswald Chamber's devotionals. One Christmas a few years back, my sister-in-law, Louise, gave me the book *Abandoned To God* by David McCasland. This book is the life story of Oswald Chambers. I enjoyed reading about one of my favorite writers and learned much from his life. Just this week, I found myself applying a lesson that I learned from that book. Louise's discipleship gift was also meaningful because it demonstrated that she was paying attention to my personal spiritual interests and growth.

Discipleship Gift: Tools for Learning

When my nephew, Jim, was fourteen, his favorite Christmas gift was a PDA, a personal digital assistant. A hand-held computer allows him to keep a calendar, task list, and names and addresses at his fingertips at all times.

Jim has always been a good student but knew he could use help getting organized. "I am very busy with my school, music, church, family, and friends. I needed the PDA because I was having trouble keeping up with everything I needed. I knew I needed help when I forgot to do a couple of key assignments in Junior High School. The PDA has made all the difference."

Knowing Jim was responsible, his family decided he needed a process for managing his time and assignments. Family members taught him some simple lessons in time management. The PDA was a tool given to him to manage his life better. It helped him to "study and show himself approved." He made straight A's on his next report card.

A normal fourteen-year-old, Jim grinned, "It also has games."

Discipleship Gift: A Warning

Recipients may not appreciate a gift of discipleship if its intent is to "fix" some problem that the family member or friend is not yet ready to deal with. Worse, they may not have even admitted they have a problem. There is a big difference between making disciples and being critical or minding someone else's business. There are three rules for giving discipleship gifts: prayer, kindness, and gentleness.

Application (5-10 Minutes)

Making It Personal

Are you spending daily time improving yourself? Do you "study and show yourself approved" spiritually and professionally? How can you improve? Are there gifts you need this Christmas that will help you improve?

_____

_____

Do you spend time every day studying the Bible and learning how to be a better disciple? How can you improve? What gifts could you use to help with this?

_____

_____

Do you love the Lord God with your entire mind? Are you strengthening that mind daily? How can you do better?

_____

_____

Commit to Jesus that you will strengthen your mind every day.

Praying Continuously (1 Thessalonians 5:17)

- As you go through your day, pay attention to your discipleship. Ask God to show you what you need to study. Did you begin your day with God? Did you have the tools you needed to study His word?
- In your profession, is there more you need to know? Notice what would help.
- Ask God to send you opportunities to model discipleship to the people around you.

Pay attention to those around you.
- Ask God to show you what they need to study.
- Resist the temptation to point out their failures.
- Pray for them, asking God for a way to make disciples of all nations.
- Remembering the rules (prayer, kindness, and gentleness), look for ways to help.

- Communicate your discipleship needs listed above to a friend or family member.

Ending The Day

- Thank God for the privilege of being His disciple.
- How was your discipleship today? If your discipleship needs improvement, confess. If you need to study more or have found yourself "ashamed of your work," confess.
- Ask God to show you ways to be a better disciple tomorrow. Ask God if you owe anyone an apology.
- Praise Him for being your teacher.

Mission Gifts

Meditation (3-5 Minutes)

Begin by being still before God. Read John 3:16 and meditate on the words "For God so loved the world, that he gave his only begotten Son, that whosoever believeth in him should not perish, but have everlasting life. For God sent not his Son into the world to condemn the world; but that the world through him might be saved." (John 3:16-17 KJV)

- Be still and know He is God.
- Do you truly believe in Jesus Christ?
    - If yes, enjoy that belief.
    - If no, ask God to help you believe.
- Think about eternal life.
    - Picture an eternity with God.
    - Picture singing with a Heavenly Host.
    - Picture your new body.
    - Think about heaven with anticipation.
- Think about why Jesus came.
    - Allow your guilt to melt away.
    - Enjoy your salvation.
- Listen to the voice of God.

Prayer (5-10 Minutes)

Appendix A: Requests of the Christ Child

- Ask God to speak to you during this devotional time.

- In Appendix A, list people who need Christ.
  - Do you know people who have never accepted Christ?
  - Do you know people who once believed but have fallen away?
- Ask God to help you have a heart for missions this Christmas.
- Prayerfully update Appendix A with new requests and answers.
- Ask for knowledge of His will for you this Christmas and the power to carry it out.
- Ask the Holy Spirit to interpret the scriptures you are about to read.

Appendix B: Gifts from the Christ Child

- Thank God for loving us and sending His son. Praise Him for the simplicity of the process for committing our lives to Him.
- In Appendix B, list:
  - Gifts you have received because you are God's child.
  - The names of loved ones that know Christ.

Appendix C: Gifts to the Christ Child

- Offer Him yourself this Christmas.
- Make a commitment to donate to a mission fund in the name of Christ and list it in Appendix C.
- Prayerfully update Appendix C.

Appendix D: Celebrations for the Christ Child

- Turn to Appendix D. Will your planned celebrations lead others to Christ? Do you need to add any events?
- Update your "To Do" list with tasks you need to delete and add.

Bible Study (10-15 Minutes)

A Christian's mission is to tell the world about Christ. Another word for mission is evangelism. It is said that our ministry is to other Christians and our mission is to the world. We love our neighbor as ourselves when we share the greatest gift we have ever received, Jesus Christ.

At Christmas, the world turns an eye and ear towards Christ. It may not be deliberate, but throughout Christmas, they honor Jesus' coming. Malls light up with Christmas lights. Stores plan campaigns around the Christmas holiday. Christmas music plays on our radios and in stores. Even non-believers attend Christmas Eve services. There is no better opportunity than Christmas to lead others toward Christ.

Background Scripture

Read Matthew 28:19-20. What do you think it means to "Go and teach all nations?"

_____

_____

We tell the world about Christ but we baptize in the name of the Father, Son, and the Holy Spirit. Describe your relationship with each of the three faces of God.

_____

_____

_____

_____

What are we supposed to do after we baptize?

_____

_____

Who is giving us this commission? _____

Like us, the disciples doubted their abilities to evangelize. Jesus made them a promise. What was it?

_____

_____

If you are willing to accept your commission this Christmas, write Jesus a letter. Let Him know you are willing to accept your commission. Tell Him your concerns and insecurities. Tell Him what distracts you from fulfilling this commission. Thank Him for His promise to be with you. Claim His power.

_____

_____

_____

_____

Read Revelation 3:20. When we tell others about Christ, we know Christ has gone before us. He is standing at the door and knocking. What is His promise to us?

_____

_____

Mission Gifts: Giving

The Southern Baptist Convention has a mission fund named after Lottie Moon, a faithful servant of God. Lottie Moon was born in the late 1800's and spent her life as a missionary to China. The Lottie Moon Christmas Offering funds much of the Baptist Missionary work all over the world. Through funds like the Lottie Moon Christmas Offering, each of us has the opportunity to share in the work of missions around the world.

James and Jennifer are a young married couple who have committed their lives to helping their world. They are missionaries in a faraway isolated place. They have made the sacrifice to leave their family and country and live far away. They are raising their two small sons across the world from their grandparents.

James and Jennifer cover a wide territory. Their car was unreliable and became a barrier to helping those around them. Through the Lottie Moon Christmas Offering, James and Jennifer received a "mostly new" van. Now they drive where they need to go without fear of their car breaking down. Those that gave money to the Lottie Moon Offering became a part of James and Jennifer's ministry.

Mission Gifts: Bibles

When I began writing this book, I asked my daughter Kelley what her favorite Christmas gift was. "That's easy. It was my Precious Moments Bible. It led me to Christ."

As background to Kelley's story, I must tell my son Chris's story. He was six and had just learned to read, so we gave him a Bible. It is a family tradition for everyone to open one gift on Christmas Eve. Chris opened his Bible. Reverently, he traced his engraved name with his fingers. He stared at the picture of Jesus holding a lamb and surrounded by children. He knew that he had received something important.

We opened the Bible to Luke and haltingly, he read the Christmas story. "Do you understand what you read?" I asked.

"Yes. God's son came to earth. Mary and Joseph took care of him."

"When you are older," I explained, "you will want to become a Christian and give your life to the Baby Jesus."

Chris, the analytical child, calmly asked, "Why do I have to wait?"

"Most people wait at least until they are eight years old or older. You will have a better understanding when you are a little older."

"What don't I understand now?" he demanded. His question caught me by surprise. I had to think. I quickly asked God for the words.

"Do you know whose son Jesus is?"

Solemnly, he nodded, "God's son."

"Why did Jesus die on the cross?"

He had already memorized John 3:16. "Jesus died so that we could live in heaven with God."

"Do you know what sin is?" I asked.

Chris liked knowing the answers. "Sin is when I do bad things."

"Have you ever sinned?" He nodded and gave a couple of examples of things mostly involving his little sister.

"Are you really ready to commit your life to Jesus?" I asked. I was worried because he was so logical and "matter of fact."

"Why would anyone decide not to commit their life to Jesus?" he asked.

Personally, I have always wondered the same thing. I attempted an answer. "Sometimes people want to do things their way instead of God's way. Some people don't believe in Jesus."

"That's silly." He insisted on moving forward with his decision.

That Christmas Eve, Chris and I prayed together as he invited Jesus into his life. As an adult, Chris remembers the experience and says he never doubted his conversion to Christianity.

Now back to Kelley. Kelley was still five when she got her fist Bible. She was in kindergarten and couldn't read. "I want a Bible," she announced.

I had planned to get her one in first grade. "Why don't we wait until you can read? You have your little New Testament to take to church." She looked stubborn. Since she loved to copy her big brother, I offered, "Chris didn't get his first Bible until he was six."

Her eyes lit up and I knew I had said the wrong thing. My competitive daughter liked getting a Bible a year younger than Chris was. "I want a Bible. You can read it to me."

While Chris was analytical and reverent, Kelley's blond head and little curls were bobbing with excitement and emotion. She couldn't wait to get her Bible. "I want to open my Bible on Christmas Eve." She was bouncing as she opened her Precious Moments Bible. "Read me the Christmas Story," she said as she handed me the Bible. She climbed in my lap so she could see the pictures.

As we read the Christmas story, I told Kelley about Chris accepting Christ when he got his first Bible. She was fascinated. "Can I do the same thing?"

"Honey, this is serious. You don't want to do this just to copy your brother. You should wait until you're older."

Kelley became indignant. "I already love Jesus! I want to invite Him into my life right this very moment."

I read her some Scripture. "Do you know what this means?" There was no doubt in my little Kelley. Five seemed young but it felt wrong not to honor her request. We knelt and prayed together. She confessed her sins, such as they were. Like Chris, her sins mostly involved picking on her sibling. She told Jesus she loved him and asked Him to be her friend.

On January 7, 1986, she talked to the pastor and told him of her decision. He was concerned that a five-year-old couldn't possibly understand her decision. She firmly announced, "I do too understand."

After many gentle questions, he said, "If you decide to 'walk the aisle' and present your decision to the church, I will joyfully baptize you. Kelley, when you get older, you might feel the need to go through this process again. Don't ever feel bad about that."

She looked him straight in the eye and said, "No I won't! I'm only doing this one time." He smiled at her enthusiasm. Kelley has loved Jesus all of her life. He became her close friend the night she got her Bible. She knows her decision for Christ was real at age five and remembers the change in her life. She never felt the need to go through the process again. She has never rethought her decision.

Kelley is now a children's minister and believes children have the capacity to turn their lives over to Christ at a young age. "Their lives will be easier if they make this important decision early." She is committed to helping them know Jesus at an early age.

As adults, Kelley and Chris are close friends. Miraculously, they no longer pick on each other. Chris has had tremendous influence on Kelley's life. That influence was apparent even when she was five years old and wanted to be just like him. In addition to her Bible, Kelley had another mission gift that Christmas. She had a godly brother who taught her how to surrender to Christ. Chris's influence on his sister has helped shape a godly adult who now also influences his life.

Celebrations become traditions when they are repeated by the next generation. Maybe one day, my grandson, Noah, will make it a tradition to accept Christ on Christmas Eve.

Mission Gifts: A Warning

Like other gifts, there are some warnings that go with giving mission gifts. Not everyone appreciates getting mission or evangelism gifts. Some think they are boring. Children usually prefer toys. Giving a Bible to someone who has made it clear that he or she does not believe in Christ may create a tense situation that becomes a barrier to future decisions.

Pray about the decision to give a mission gift. I know several people who were led to Christ by Bibles that made them angry when they received them. I also know other people who say they are not a Christian because family members "shoved it into their faces."

Application (5-10 Minutes)

Making It Personal

Have you given gifts, money, or time this Christmas for leading our world to Christ? Why or why not?

_____

_____

Have people close to you rejected Christ or the Bible? Have they been delaying a decision to accept Christ? Get on your knees right now and pray for them. Ask God what you can do for them this Christmas. Write His response to your prayer.

_____

_____

Is there a gift you need that will help you personally with missions?

_____

_____

Praying Continuously (1 Thessalonians 5:17)

- At mealtimes and bedtime, pray for people to find Christ this Christmas. As you interact with people:
  - Ask yourself, do I know if they are Christians?
  - Ask God what you can do to tell them about Christ.
- Communicate your ministry gift needs listed above to a friend or family member.

Ending The Day

Did you tell the world about Christ? If not, confess. Ask God for His power to do better tomorrow.

Worship Gifts

Meditation (3-5 Minutes)

Begin by being still before God. Meditate on the words "Make a joyful noise unto the LORD, all ye lands. Serve the LORD with gladness: come before his presence with singing. Know ye that the LORD he is God: it is he that hath made us, and not we ourselves; we are his people, and the sheep of his pasture. Enter into his gates with thanksgiving, and into his courts with praise: be thankful unto him, and bless his name. For the LORD is good; his mercy is everlasting; and his truth endureth to all generations." (Psalm 100 KJV)

- Be still and know He is God.
- Make a joyful noise unto the Lord.
- Come before His presence with singing.
- He made us. Enjoy being His. Give thanks to Him.
- We are the sheep of His pasture. Listen to His voice.
- Enter into His gates with thanksgiving and His courts with praise.
- For the Lord is God. Enjoy His mercy.
- Listen to His truth, which endures for all generations.
- Listen to the voice of God.

Prayer (5-10 Minutes)

Appendix A: Requests of the Christ Child

- Ask God to speak to you during this devotional time.
- Do you want to worship? Do you wake up in the morning with a yearning to worship God? Ask God to teach you how to worship.

- Do you worship God before you "open your treasures" and give Christmas gifts? Ask Him to give you a heart for Him this Christmas.
- Turn to Appendix A and ask God to help you worship as you give your gifts. Pray and update.
- Ask for knowledge of His will for you this Christmas and the power to carry it out.
- Ask the Holy Spirit to interpret the scriptures you are about to read.

Appendix B: Gifts from the Christ Child

- Praise our God, The Most High, for loving us. Tell Him how much you love Him.
- Turn to Appendix B and thank your Heavenly Father for the privilege of worship.

Appendix C: Gifts to the Christ Child

- Offer your worship to Christ.
- Turn to Appendix C and lay each gift at the feet of the Baby Jesus, and worship. Pray and update Appendix C.

Appendix D: Celebrations for the Christ Child

- Turn to Appendix D. Put a W by the events that are for worship.
- Update your "To Do" list, praying about each action.

Bible Study (10-15 Minutes)

At Christmas, we have two choices. We can worship the gifts we give or we can give our gifts in worship. The title of this Devotion is "Worship Gifts." Are you giving "worship gifts" or do you worship "gifts?"

We are worshiping gifts when we "chase after gifts." Are you frantically running through malls, feeling pressure to spend too much money or at least as much as someone else does? Do you overspend at Christmas, resent gift giving, or are you stingy? Do you feel resentment about what you receive at Christmas? When Christmas is over, are you left wanting "more" or dealing with the reality of overwhelming Christmas bills? If you have answered yes to a majority of these questions, you may be worshiping gifts. Write a letter of confession to God, asking for help.

_____

_____

_____

_____

If you have been worshiping gifts, you are in the majority. There is hope. God can overcome our human nature and replace it with His.

Do you pray about your gifts and offer them to the Christ Child? Do you enjoy giving and receiving? Do you "open your treasures" and give with a cheerful heart? Do you give only what you can truly afford? Do you feel a sense of peace and satisfaction when the Christmas season is past? If so, you are probably worshiping God and not gifts. Write a letter of thanksgiving.

_____

_____

_____

_____

We love God with our souls when we worship Him. Worship gifts are the final category of gifts we will discuss in this devotional series. Worship gifts are those gifts that assist us with our worship of God.

Background Scripture

Have you ever bought an extravagant gift for Christmas, only to have it break immediately? Read Isaiah 1:22-23. What does our silver and wine turn into when we "chase after gifts"?

_____

Read 2 Chronicles 31:14. We are worshiping God with our gifts when we think of these gifts as "consecrated contributions" made to the Lord. The dictionary definition of consecrated is "to dedicate solely to a purpose or a goal" (www.dictionary.com). What is the goal of your gift giving this Christmas? Are your gifts consecrated?

_____

_____

2 Corinthians 9:7 is a model for how to give gifts. First, each man (or woman) should decide in his heart what to give. We are not to give reluctantly or under compulsion. What kind of giver does God love?

_____

Read Psalm 96:9. As you give gifts this Christmas, worship the Lord in the splendor of His holiness.

Personal Examples of Worship Gifts

I keep a daily prayer journal. In this journal, I write love letters to God and keep a list of prayer requests and their answers. I keep another list of people I know who need to know Jesus Christ personally. Over the years, people have given me many journals. Because I keep filling them up, I always enjoy a new journal. These journals assist my daily private worship.

In addition to writing, I worship through music. People occasionally give me Christian music books and sheet music. I enjoy using these books while worshiping quietly at the piano. Much of my worship is in the car with Christian CDs, and I always love new CDs.

Some gifts actually remind me to worship. Our children gave us a quilt for our 30th wedding anniversary. This quilt is special because it has their pictures on it. It hangs on a stairway wall. I pray for my family as I pass this quilt multiple times per day. This quilt has become an instrument of worship.

Worship Gifts for a Worship Leader

At 14 my nephew, Jim, said he loved Christmas because he enjoyed worshiping God with Christmas carols. He preferred singing from the hymnal because he enjoyed singing parts. Jim's understanding of the true meaning of Christmas was clear from his remark, "We celebrate Christmas because God sent His Son to earth. Now *that* is something to sing about."

Jim met Jesus personally as a very young child. I asked him, "Do you remember what you were like before you knew Jesus?"

"Yes," he answered. "Right after I became a Christian, I was very aware of the difference between right and wrong. Suddenly I felt a real desire to do the right thing. I even wanted to treat my younger brother better." I shook my head as I laughed. Our family really needs work on how we treat our siblings.

"Many adults who accept Jesus as a young child forget what it was like to be without Christ. Do you think you'll ever forget?" I asked.

"I won't forget because I made a decision to remember. I think most people remember what they decide to remember."

Jim was a musician and attended a School of the Arts High School. He was a pianist, singer, and guitarist. While Jim was smart and talented, he had to practice. Between his piano and guitar, he spent several hours a day learning to play skillfully.

A couple of years before, Jim's family gave him his bass guitar as a Christmas gift. My husband, Bob, (Jim's uncle) played the bass and used the skill as a worship leader in his church. Bob taught him a little about the bass and Jim taught himself the rest. Then, Jim used his skills as a worship leader in his own church. Only 14, he began playing his bass guitar every Sunday during the morning worship service.

Jim says, "I love participating in the worship service. The only thing I mind is not being able to sing along with the hymns. At least I get to go to our Sunday evening worship and sing there."

As Jim talked, I thought of Psalm 57:7-8: "My heart is steadfast, O God, my heart is steadfast; I will sing and make music. Awake, my soul! Awake, harp and lyre! I will awaken the dawn" (NIV). Jim sang and made music with a "steadfast heart."

Read Psalm 33:2-3. How is Jim following this Scripture?

_____

_____

Warnings about Worshiping Gifts

Like the other types of gifts, there are warnings that go with giving "worship gifts." Not everyone knows how to worship. They may not know how to use the gift they receive. If helping with worship is the purpose of a gift you give, be prepared to teach the recipient how to use it.

Not everyone wants to worship. People may not appreciate your gift. Worse, people may think you are trying to control their behavior. Remember that most people worship gifts. Think about it. It's hard to worship a gift that has the purpose of worship.

The last warning is that not everyone worships the same way. Something useful to you may not be useful to everyone.

Application (5-10 Minutes)

Making It Personal

Write a letter to God, worshiping Him.

_____

_____

_____

_____

Think about a gift you received last year. Using the example of Jim's bass guitar, how could you have better used your gift to assist with worship?

_____

_____

Ask our Wonderful Counselor if any of the gifts you have received in the past could become a worship gift. Write His answer below.

_____

_____

Is there a gift you need that will help you personally with worship?

_____

_____

Praying Continuously (1 Thessalonians 5:17)

- Look around your home. Find gifts that people have given you. Find a way to use them for the purpose of worship. Examples:
    - A Picture—If someone has given you a picture, take a moment and thank God for that person. Pray for their families, teachers, doctors, and employers.
    - A Bike—Take a ride. Praise God for everything you see. Breathe in His fresh air and feel His presence. Feel His wind on your face and let His Spirit freshen your spirit.
    - Apparel—If you are wearing something someone gave you, pray for the person who gave it to you.
- Communicate your worship gift needs listed above to a friend or family member.

Ending The Day

- Think about your day.
    - If you worshiped gifts, confess.
    - If you received gifts, praise Him.
- Praise God for the privilege of giving Him gifts this Christmas. Ask Him what He wants for Christmas.

The Christmas Stars

Meditation (3-5 Minutes)

Begin by being still before God. Meditate on the words "Search me, O God, and know my heart: try me, and know my thoughts: And see if there be any wicked way in me, and lead me in the way everlasting." (Psalm 139:23-24 KJV)

- Be still and know He is God.
- Sit quietly and let God search you and know your heart.
  - Give God your anxious thoughts.
  - Offer God any offensive way in you.
- Listen as God leads you in the way everlasting.
- Listen to the voice of God.

Prayer (5-10 Minutes)

Appendix A: Requests of the Christ Child

- Ask God to speak to you during this devotional time.
- Ask God to show you the role He has planned for you this Christmas. Ask God to remove anything that is blocking you from fulfilling that role.
- Think about the roles you play at Christmas for your family, church, and employer. Turn to Appendix A and list each role (parent, child, church member, etc.). Ask for help.
- Ask for knowledge of His will for you this Christmas and the power to carry it out.
- Ask the Holy Spirit to interpret the scriptures you are about to read.

Appendix B: Gifts from the Christ Child

- Thank God for Christmas.
    - For the first Christmas.
    - For this Christmas.
    - For all the Christmases in the middle.
- Think about the things other people do for you at Christmas.
    - Thank God for the people who play a role in your Christmas.
    - Turn to Appendix B and list them as a Christmas blessing.

Appendix C: Gifts to the Christ Child

- Offer yourself to Christ this Christmas.
- Offer to be His servant at home.
- Offer to be His servant at church.
- Offer to be His servant in your place of employment.
- Offer to be His servant in the world.
- Turn to Appendix C and list anything that comes to mind. Pray and update.

Appendix D: Celebrations for the Christ Child

- Turn to Appendix D and study your celebrations. Think about the roles you are playing. Is there anything you need to add to your "To Do" list to better play your role?
- Update your "To Do" list, praying about each action.

Bible Study (10-15 Minutes)

God was the director of the first Christmas. He promoted the event for centuries. In fact, people had heard about it for so long that many forgot to look for it. God himself played three starring roles. As Father, He planned His family. He picked a mother for His son. He sent a messenger to tell her the good news. As Holy Spirit, He came upon this special young woman and the "Power of the Most High" overshadowed her so the Holy One could be born. As Jesus, He came as a baby to save the world.

God selected the rest of His cast carefully. He used ordinary people in the process of living their lives. He used priests, world leaders, and astronomers. Some played the role of "Good Guy" and some "Bad Guy." God even allowed angels to star in His production.

Background Scripture

Open your Bible to the books of Luke and Matthew. There were many roles played in this first Christmas production. Below, we will examine the personality and character traits of the stars from the very first Christmas. As you read briefly about each star, write what you think he or she was like. For example, Mary was bright, inquisitive, humble, fearful, and obedient. Zechariah was righteous and faithful. He had a servant's heart but a stubborn head. As you write about each person, think about your own personality and character traits. Who are you like? Could God have used you in His production?

Angel Gabriel

Read Luke 1:13 and Luke 1:30. Describe the nature of God's chosen angel.

_____

_____

Read Luke 1:19-20. Gabriel was kind but no wimp. Zechariah confronted Gabriel and demanded evidence of his words. Describe how Gabriel responded. On whose authority did he act? What "proof" did he give Zechariah?

_____

_____

Elizabeth and Zechariah

Read Luke 1:6. Describe Elizabeth and Zechariah's character. Who were they? What kind of people did God choose to give birth to the forerunner of His son?

_____

_____

Were Elizabeth and Zechariah perfect? What mistakes did they make?

_____

_____

Mary the Mother

Read Luke 1:26-30 and 46-55. To her friends and family, Mary may have seemed ordinary but we know Mary was extraordinary. What kind of woman did God choose to mother His son?

_____

_____

Joseph

Read Matthew 1:19, 24. Poor Joseph. Imagine his agony when he found the love of his life, Mary, was expecting. Describe him and his response to this difficult news.

_____

_____

The Shepherds

Read Luke 2:8-20. What kind of men were the shepherds? How do you think they dressed? What economic level do you think they represented? How did they respond to God's instructions?

_____

_____

Simeon

Read Luke 2:25-36. Another simple priest played a humble and prophetic role in God's production. What was Simeon like?

_____

_____

Prophetess Anna

Read Luke 2:36-38. What role did Anna play? What do you think she was like? Why do you think we read about Anna in the Bible?

_____

_____

King Herod

Read Matthew 2:3-5, 7-8, 16. Every good story has to have a "Bad Guy." Describe the "Bad Guy" of the very first Christmas.

_____

_____

The Wise Men

Read Matthew 2:1, 9-12. Here, we see God using people who were very different from the other stars. Their race, religion, and culture were probably different from that of Mary and Joseph. What were the Wise Men like?

_____

_____

God's Christmas productions did not end with the very first Christmas. There have been over 2,000 sequels. Christians have celebrated the birth of Jesus for over 2,000 years. Year after year, people from each generation play a role in their own Christmas production. Our good guys have names like St. Nicholas, Mother Teresa, and Lottie Moon. Modern day bad guys may resemble "The Grinch" or leaders of terrorist countries or organizations.

We celebrate Christmas because we have been given a Savior called Christ the Lord. We are blessed by the presence of the Holy Spirit. In our Father's eyes, we are perfect. God gives us so much. "To whom much is given, much is required." (Luke 12:48) What is your role this Christmas?

_____

_____

Application (5-10 Minutes)

Making It Personal

Which of the stars from the first Christmas production are you most like? Are you a good guy or a bad guy? Are you a combination of several or are you like none of them?

_____

_____

Think about your Christmases. Who were the "Good Guys and Bad Guys"?

_____

_____

- Praise God for the "Good Guys."
- Ask God to help you forgive the "Bad Guys."

Are you worthy to play a role in God's production of "This Christmas?" What would make you more worthy?

_____

_____

Are you willing to play a role in God's production of "This Christmas?" What role is he casting you for? Remember that each year, the roles may change. Listen to God and think outside the box. God seldom asks the expected.

_____

_____

Praying Continuously (1 Thessalonians 5:17)

- Every time you see the color red, thank God for His production of the first Christmas.
- Every time you see the color green, ask God to reveal your role in this Christmas.

Ending The Day

- On this day, did you play a role in this Christmas?
- Were you a "Good Guy" or "Bad Guy"?
- If necessary, confess and ask forgiveness.
- Ask God if you owe anyone an apology.
- Think about the things other people did for you today. Praise God for them.

The Shepherd of Our Souls

Meditation (3-5 Minutes)

Begin by being still before God. Read Psalm 23:1-3 and meditate on the words "The LORD is my shepherd; I shall not want. He maketh me to lie down in green pastures: he leadeth me beside the still waters. He restoreth my soul: he leadeth me in the paths of righteousness for his name's sake."

- Be still and know He is God.
- Picture yourself in a field with the Lord as your shepherd.
    - He tells you where to go.
    - He protects you.
    - He meets all your needs.
    - He watches you as you sleep.
- Enjoy the green pastures.
- Kneel beside quiet water.
    - Let Him restore your soul.
    - Listen as He guides you in paths of righteousness for His name's sake.
- Listen to the voice of God.

Prayer (5-10 Minutes)

Appendix A: Requests of the Christ Child

- Ask God to speak to you during this devotional time.
- Ask God to be your shepherd.

- Ask Him to send people to shepherd and guide you.
- Ask God to make you worthy to be a shepherd for his flock.
- Turn to Appendix A and list anyone you are "shepherding."
- Pray and update Appendix A.
- Ask for knowledge of His will for you this Christmas and the power to carry it out.
- Ask the Holy Spirit to interpret the scriptures you are about to read.

Appendix B: Gifts from the Christ Child

- Thank Jesus Christ for being the shepherd of your soul.
- Think about the people who have shepherded you (your spiritual mentors).
  - Praise God for them.
  - Turn to Appendix B and list their names.

Appendix C: Gifts to the Christ Child

- Offer your services to God this Christmas, tending His flock.
- Turn to Appendix C and list any shepherding gifts you can perform for people. Pray and update.

Appendix D: Celebrations for the Christ Child

- Turn to Appendix D. Whom can you "shepherd" by inviting them to your Christmas celebrations? Put them on your "To Do" list.
- Update your "To Do" list, praying about each action.

Bible Study (10-15 Minutes)

Shepherds are an important part of God's message for us. The words shepherd and shepherds are in the Bible 100 times. The words flock and flocks are in the Bible 200 times. Consider the following shepherds:

- Adam and Eve's son, Abel, was a shepherd.
- At one time in his life, Moses "tended flocks."
- King David began his career as a shepherd. Later, God called him to "shepherd" his people. David wrote the words, "The Lord is my Shepherd."
- Shepherds were part of the first Christmas. They spread the word that our Savior was born.

When you think about it, calling us "sheep" is not very flattering. While sheep might look cute, they have "issues." They always need a shepherd. Even with a shepherd, they wander off and get lost. Alone, they starve. Although sheep have been known to be ornery and bite, they have no defense against wolves.

But alas, look around. Everywhere, we see lost and confused people. Homeless people wander the streets. We bite each other through our petty squabbles and our wars. The newspaper tells of a woman trampled while shopping a Christmas sale. We read of a fight breaking out over a Christmas present. Yes, we do need a shepherd this Christmas. Jesus is our Shepherd and we, his flock. Jesus instructs us to become shepherds ourselves and lead people to Jesus. This Christmas, tend His flock.

Background Scripture

Read Psalm 32:1. Who is your shepherd? Write this verse.

_____

_____

Think about David tending sheep. He is sitting on the hill, playing his harp and singing praises to God. He has just sung the words, "The Lord is my shepherd." Suddenly a wolf appears and goes after the sheep. What do you think David does? How much risk will he take to save his sheep?

_____

_____

Read John 10:11. Jesus calls himself the Good Shepherd. What does a good shepherd do for his sheep?

_____

_____

How was Jesus a "Good Shepherd" for us?

_____

_____

Read the prayer in Hebrews 13:20-21. A Good Shepherd also guides his sheep and meets their needs. Write the promises in these verses.

_____

_____

Read 1 Peter 5:2. Many have difficulty recognizing the hand of God. It is easier to see God working through people. Knowing this, God sends us people to shepherd us. He asks us to "shepherd" his sheep. What should our attitude be as we tend God's flock?

_____

_____

Read 1 Peter 2:25. God is the "Shepherd of our Soul." Why do we need shepherds?

_____

_____

Servants that Shepherd

Jim and Linda Gandy have been my Sunday School teachers for many years. Jim accepted Christ at age 11 and Linda at age 22. While they exercise many spiritual gifts, their primary gift is service. They "shepherd" our class with that gift.

Jim is a deacon in our church and he and Linda head up our church's "Willing Hands Ministry." "Willing Hands" provides assistance wherever people need help. Many of the people they minister to are elderly. "Willing Hands" may drive someone to the doctor, pick up medication, or make necessary home repairs. When someone has a need, he or she calls the church office or Jim and Linda.

"Our job is to match the need with an available resource. We find someone in the church that has both the necessary skill set and the willingness to help," Jim said. Many times, Jim and Linda meet the need themselves. They run errands and act as an advocate for people who cannot otherwise help themselves.

Their faith is a model for the entire class. I remember one particularly difficult year for them. This was the year Jim's mother died. "She was ready to go home to be with her Lord, but we were not ready to let her go. We tried to be joyful, but we missed her." I watched as they continued serving through their grief and the business of closing her affairs.

Not long after losing Jim's mother, Jim and Linda had to face another trial. Just before Jim's mother passed away, Jim's daughter got pregnant. "We had almost given up on being grandparents," Jim told the class. Not long after Jim's mother died, their daughter miscarried.

Knowing what wonderful grandparents they would make, we grieved the loss of that child. Jim and Linda took comfort that their grandchild is "happier than the living" and will never "see evil." (Ecclesiastes 4:1-3)

Amazingly, Jim and Linda continued their ministry through their grief. My husband had surgery a couple of days after they lost their grandchild. I was amazed when they came to the hospital and sat with me. "What are you doing here?" I asked. "You are supposed to be taking care of yourself."

I will always remember Linda's words. "The way we care for ourselves is to care for others." What a lesson that was for me. The circumstances of their lives did not cause them to lose focus. They offered their willingness to God and continued to "shepherd." By shepherding others, they allowed God to minister to their grieving souls.

As I write this, Jim and Linda are ministering to a family whose child is gravely ill. They have been faithful throughout the discouraging years of this child's physical decline. They have regularly visited the hospital, even when the child was hospitalized in other cities. They take turns sitting with the child to give the mother much-needed breaks. Through their leadership, church members have remembered to pray, helped build a wheelchair ramp, visited the hospital and home, and met other needs. Jim and Linda have taught our church how to remain faithful when God's will is confusing and our hearts are breaking. Through it all, Jim and Linda have managed to make sure Jesus and His church get the credit for their "shepherding."

I asked Jim to tell me about a meaningful Christmas he experienced. Before teaching adults, Jim taught youth. "One Christmas, my Senior High class decided to gather gifts for a needy family. Their purpose was to demonstrate love and concern. The youth got excited and did a wonderful job. They collected many, many gifts. Our next goal was to locate a family and provide their children with gifts. Surprisingly, we could not find a needy family. Our gifts had no recipients. The youth were disappointed and began to feel they had wasted their time. They even questioned God and actually lost some of their purpose and reason for giving. Just two days before Christmas, a desperate church member called. She needed gifts for the foster children she was keeping. She was an elderly woman with a lot of love and not much money. She was broken hearted that she could not afford to give Christmas gifts to these children. The church immediately called us. I called my youth. On Christmas Eve, we took the gifts over to the home. There we experienced the real meaning of Christmas."

Through the Holy Spirit and the guidance of these gentle shepherds, these youth learned many lessons. They learned the lesson of giving through faith. By giving, they met a faithful woman who had little economically, but gave all she had. Like the Wise Men, she "opened her treasures" and gave to these foster children (Matthew 2:11). This foster mother may not have had the economic "treasures" of the Wise Men, but her gifts were just as valuable. One of her "treasures" was her church family. She trusted God and God provided for her needs through her church.

The youth learned about "waiting on God." The Holy Spirit led them to collect the gifts. He waited before providing a recipient for those gifts. His waiting taught the youth to trust God's plan and timing. As the saying goes, God is never late but He is seldom early.

They learned how to fill their pockets with the blessing of making a difference. It was a Christmas the youth would never forget. Jim's gift of service to this family was the gifts they received. His gift of service to the youth was to "shepherd" them into trusting and following "The Shepherd of our Soul."

Application (5-10 Minutes)

Making It Personal

Write a letter to Jesus thanking Him for being the "Shepherd of our Soul." Thank Him for sending us shepherds to guide us. Praise Him for the privilege of caring for His flock this Christmas.

_____

_____

_____

_____

Are you shepherding others this Christmas? Is God leading you to do something specific? Make a commitment.

_____

_____

Think about the shepherds in your life. How are you allowing them to shepherd you?

_____

_____

Think about the needs in your life. Do you need to lie down in the "green pastures"? How are you letting the "Great Shepherd" minister to you?

_____

_____

Praying Continuously (1 Thessalonians 5:17)

- As you go through your day, notice the people who "shepherd" you. Praise God for them, even if you find yourself unreceptive to their "help."
    - Is your manager asking you to make some kind of change?
    - Are co-workers pushing you to do more?
    - Is your spouse offering "helpful" suggestions?
    - Is someone at your church holding you accountable?
- Today, find something to do for someone else.
    - Make sure no one knows of your good deed.
    - It can be something small or large.
    - Allow Jesus to shepherd your soul.
    - Pray about what you are to do.
    - Follow through on what He tells you.

Ending The Day

- Thank our heavenly Shepherd for sending us shepherds like Jim and Linda. Thank God for the shepherds in your life.
    - Are you humble enough to allow them to shepherd you?
    - If not, confess and ask for help.
- Examine your own life.
    - If you are not being a "shepherd," confess to "The Great Shepherd."
    - Pray for the people you are shepherding.

Christmas Lights

Meditation (3-5 Minutes)

Begin by being still before God. Meditate on the words "Send forth your light and your truth, let them guide me; let them bring me to your holy mountain, to the place where you dwell. Then will I go to the altar of God, to God, my joy and my delight. I will praise you with the harp, O God, my God." (Psalm 43:3-4 NIV)

- Be still and know He is God.
- As you sit quietly, let Him send forth his "Light and Truth."
    - Let His light and truth guide you.
    - Let Him bring you to His "Holy Mountain" where He dwells.
    - Go to "The Altar" of your "Joy" and "Delight."
- Finish your meditation singing praises to God.
- Listen to the voice of God.

Prayer (5-10 Minutes)

Appendix A: Requests of the Christ Child

- Ask God to speak to you during this devotional time.
- Ask Jesus to light your way this Christmas.
    - If your eyes feel dark, kneel before God and ask to see the world with His eyes.
    - Ask Him to help you light the way for His children.
- Appendix A: Pray and update.
- Ask for knowledge of His will for you this Christmas and the power to carry it out.
- Ask the Holy Spirit to interpret the scriptures you are about to read.

Appendix B: Gifts from the Christ Child

- Thank God:
    - For the Christmas lights you see everywhere.
    - For sending us Jesus, the Light of the World.
- In Appendix B, list the people who are lights in your life.

Appendix C: Gifts to the Christ Child

- Offer yourself as a Christmas light for Jesus.
- Ask God to make you a light as you give gifts this Christmas.
- Appendix C: Pray and update.

Appendix D: Celebration for the Christ Child

- Turn to Appendix D and update your "To Do" list.
- As you begin attending celebrations, notice the Christmas lights involved.

Bible Study (10-15 Minutes)

Remember a time when the lights of your house went out. How did you get around? Did you bump into furniture as you frantically looked for a flashlight or candle? Were you feeling your way across a room, which would have been easily crossable only moments before? When you finally lit that flashlight or candle, was there a sense of relief as a tiny beam pierced your darkness?

Now remember how you felt when the lights finally came back on. As light flooded the entire room, did you feel a sense of freedom with the limitations removed? What impact did that light have on you?

Some people live in spiritual darkness. They stumble from situation to situation, feeling their way along the wall. They live with bruises, pain, and broken bones. Some remember a time when they had light but now have lost their way. For others, darkness has consumed their entire life.

Some spend their life carrying a tiny candle or flashlight. Since they can see, they think it is enough. They see those in total darkness and feel fortunate in comparison. They go through life only half living. They do not know what a room flooded with light would be like. They may know Jesus as Savior but have never met Him as a close friend and counselor. Their small beam of light is gradually burning down.

In a world of darkness, pain, and evil, God sent Jesus Christ to light the way. If we choose, we can see the world with His eyes. When we see with His eyes, the room is flooded with light.

Fear is gone. We see our blessings in all circumstances. When difficulties come, Jesus' light gives us peace and understanding.

Christmas lights symbolize the light of Jesus. They remind us of His love. We see them in shopping malls, on houses, and in church. As Christians, we are to let the light of Jesus show through us. This Christmas, light the darkness for those around you.

Background Scripture

Read Genesis 1:3-4. God invented light. As He looked around, what was his opinion of light? Do you agree with His assessment?

_____

_____

Read Psalm 27:1. Who is the Lord? Write this entire Scripture. Say it aloud. Believe it.

_____

_____

Read Matthew 4:16. Without the light of Jesus, what land do people live in? Do you know anyone who lives in this land?

_____

_____

Read Proverbs 13:9. Is your lamp burning? What happens to the lamp of the wicked?

_____

_____

Read Jesus' words in Matthew 6:14-16. What are we supposed to do with our lamps?

_____

_____

Read Acts 20:35. At Christmas, we have an opportunity to be the light of the world. We can give blessings to others. What does the Scripture say about giving?

_____

_____

Read Matthew 6:22-23. The eye is the lamp of our body. What happens if our eyes are good?

_____

_____

What happens if our eyes are bad?

_____

_____

The Night People

Read the Scripture below. Listen carefully to Jesus' warning from John 3:19-21 (NIV):

"This is the verdict: Light has come into the world, but men loved darkness instead of light because their deeds were evil. Everyone who does evil hates the light, and will not come into the light for fear that his deeds will be exposed. But whoever lives by the truth comes into the light, so that it may be seen plainly that what he has done has been done through God."

My adopted son, David, was one of a group of people I call "The Night People." "Night People" are those who stay up all night playing and sleep off their derelictions during the day. I am not talking about people who work night shifts. I am talking about people who do things most can't imagine. A cloak of darkness shrouds their deeds as their pockets are full of the night. David was born to a family of "Night People." I first met him when he was six years old and his abusive dysfunctional biological family had abandoned him. He moved in with us and we later adopted him.

David fought darkness. Our first Christmas with David found him dazed and baffled by a room full of toys. Never before had Santa Claus visited him. Worse, he had never heard the name Jesus. When we told him the real meaning of Christmas, he accepted Jesus right away. He sat in church wide eyed, listening to every word, clinging to me. We had such hopes for him.

David teetered between two worlds. He made dire mistakes, confessed, and improved for long periods. Then, he would do something that shocked everyone around him. His deeds included theft, starting fires, putting glass in a neighbor's shoes, and countless lies. He asked me one time, "Mama, am I just plain bad? Why do I do these things?"

"No Sweetie, people just didn't take care of you the way they should have. Now it's up to you to change." I tried to explain grace to David, but he made the same mistakes repeatedly.

When David became a teenager, he abandoned the light completely. He began staying out until the middle of the night while we searched frantically for him. His activities were dangerous, illegal, and immoral. We tried everything, but the strength of the darkness was too much. At 19, he slept entirely through Christmas Day. We waited as long as we could and finally opened gifts without him. The night had taken away his day.

David finally found the Light. A year before he died of AIDS, he called home. "Mama, I have found God again. I feel so clean." We had a glorious year almost to the day. We celebrated every holiday, anniversary and special occasion during that year except one... he died just before Father's Day. I treasure the gifts he gave that year. He knew he was dying and made each one special. He died respected by his employer and surrounded by godly friends.

One night as I was panicking over his high fever, he comforted me by saying, "Mama, I'm going to die. You have to accept that. Please don't worry about me. God has shown me where I am going." On June 8, 1995, my baby went home to the Light.

The Day People

Day people are those who work hard, love God, and do the best they can. They're not perfect nor are their lives. They have an eternal view of life and wear the world as a loose garment. They rely on God, their church, and their families to help meet their needs. They struggle but look to God for answers. Read Jesus' words in John 8:12. What is the promise?

_____

_____

My friend, Cindy, told me her favorite Christmas story. As I listened, I knew I was listening to a story about a family and church of "Day People." Ten-year-old Cindy and her younger sisters were concerned about Christmas. The girls expected it to be the worst ever. Their daddy had been sick and unemployed for over a year. "Our parents warned us that they didn't have any money. We didn't expect gifts. The worst part was that we couldn't give gifts to our grandma and cousins. I couldn't imagine Christmas without giving gifts."

"We couldn't even afford a Christmas tree. Daddy took us to the woods and we chopped down a small unimpressive pine tree. It was so much fun. We were bursting with excitement as we brought it home and decorated it. Suddenly, our living room looked like Christmas. To this day, I believe this was the most beautiful tree our family has ever had."

Cindy continued her story. "Our church found out we didn't have any money. Individual church members adopted each girl and the gifts started pouring in. We had more gifts than ever and realized we had enough to share with the rest of the family. We were worried that we had nothing to give our cousins, who were all boys. Amazingly, some of the gifts worked for little boys so we wrapped them up and gave them away."

"We all worried about Grandma," Cindy continued. "We had gifts for everyone but her. I felt terrible. Then, Daddy heard a noise in the barn and went to investigate. Hiding in the barn was a possum. Grandma loved to eat possum. Daddy trapped that possum and gave it live to Grandma the next morning. She was thrilled. She said it was the best Christmas gift she ever received." After Christmas, the entire family enjoyed a possum dinner. Like the ram God provided to Abraham so many years ago, God provided a possum for Grandma.

Those In The Middle

Many and possibly most can't make up their mind about the category in which they belong. They want to be in the light but they refuse to heed the warnings about the darkness. They believe they can live in both worlds. Read Jesus' words in Luke 16:13. What is the warning about serving two masters?

_____

_____

No one wakes up one day and decides to become a "Night Person." It happens gradually, one compromise at a time. It may start with a Saturday night party and too much to drink. On Sunday, the head hurts and going to church seems impossible. It may start with being too busy and working into the night. Exhaustion becomes an excuse for skipping devotions and worship services.

John grew up in church. He became a Christian at an early age. His values and ethics were strong. He was a leader in his church and school. Then, John went off to college. The first thing that happened was that he stopped going to church. He did not know anyone and it was easier to sleep in on Sunday. He rationalized that he would go to church when he was at home.

John's friends were artists and musicians who had creative philosophies about life. They offered these philosophies, listening to music, until way into the night. They began influencing John's thoughts. Doubts crept in. John fought his doubts but didn't discuss them with anyone who would tell him the truth.

Gradually, John began making moral compromises. He rationalized that everyone occasionally overindulged in food or alcohol. The people around him took light drugs and he occasionally experimented. He abandoned his vow of celibacy before marriage. Needing to rationalize his new behavior, he began considering himself "enlightened." John no longer believes in Christianity, thinking it too limiting. He has lost his faith.

Gradually, the night is taking away John's days. He parties until late into the night and claims to have lost interest in material things. That translates into his having trouble earning money and his family feeling obligated to help. John is living in that space between the night and the day, rapidly moving toward the night.

None of us can stay still. We are either walking into brighter light or headed toward the darkness. Jesus is the Truth and Light. He tells Christians to radiate His light. This Christmas, walk toward the light.

Application (5-10 Minutes)

Making It Personal

How are your "eyes" during this Christmas season? Are they full of light? Do you see God's blessings everywhere? Write a praise letter to God.

_____

_____

_____

_____

Are your eyes full of darkness? Are you only seeing what is wrong with the world and your life? Write a letter of confession, asking God for his help.

_____

_____

_____

_____

Are you:

- A day person?
- A night person?
- Somewhere in between?

How are you lighting the world for others this Christmas? Could your lamp burn brighter?

_____

_____

Praying Continuously (1 Thessalonians 5:17)

- Notice the Christmas lights. Each time you see a Christmas light:
  - Praise God for being your Light.
  - Ask to be able to see the world through His eyes.

Ending The Day

- Did you walk toward the Light today? Praise God for His Light.
- Did you walk toward the darkness today? Confess and ask for forgiveness.

The Family of God

Meditation (3-5 Minutes)

Begin by being still before God. Meditate on the words "For this cause I bow my knees unto the Father of our Lord Jesus Christ, of whom the whole family in heaven and earth is named, that he would grant you, according to the riches of his glory, to be strengthened with might by his Spirit in the inner man; that Christ may dwell in your hearts by faith; that ye, being rooted and grounded in love, may be able to comprehend with all saints what is the breadth, and length, and depth, and height; and to know the love of Christ, which passeth knowledge, that ye might be filled with all the fullness of God." (Ephesians 3:14-19 KJV).

- Be still and know He is God.
- Kneel before the Father.
    - Think of your entire family in heaven and earth.
    - God is your Father.
    - His children are your brothers and sisters.
    - Enjoy being in God's family.
    - Let His glorious riches strengthen your inner being.
    - Let Christ dwell in your heart.
    - Meditate on how wide, long, high, and deep Christ's love is for you.
    - Let the fullness of God fill you.
- Listen to the voice of God.

Prayer (5-10 Minutes)

Appendix A - Requests of the Christ Child

- Ask God to speak to you during this devotional time.
- Ask God to help you to be a good "family member" this Christmas:
    - In the home.
    - In the church.
    - In the world.
- If your home is troubled, write a prayer in Appendix A.
- If you are dreading any family celebrations this Christmas, write a prayer in Appendix A.
- Pray and update Appendix A with any requests or answers.
- Ask for knowledge of His will for you this Christmas and the power to carry it out.
- Ask the Holy Spirit to interpret the scriptures you are about to read.

Appendix B - Gifts from the Christ Child

- Thank God for the family fellowship offered during the Christmas Season.
- Turn to Appendix B and list family members for whom you are grateful.
    - At home.
    - In church.
    - In the world.

Appendix C - Gifts to the Christ Child

- This Christmas, offer to God:
    - Your love.
    - Yourself.
- Ask Him what other gifts you're to give your family this Christmas.
- Pray and update Appendix C.

Appendix D – Celebration for the Christ Child

- Turn to Appendix D and pray for the people with whom you will be celebrating.
    - Think of them as family.
    - As a family member, is there anything you need to add to your "To Do" list?

Bible Study (10-15 Minutes)

The word "family" is in the Bible 175 times. We see families working, worshiping, and living together. The Bible offers stories of family love, as well as stories of betrayal. God created Eve so Adam would not be alone and we all know where that led poor Adam. To save his life, Moses' mother gently placed him in a basket among the bulrushes in the river as his big sister tenderly watched him. At the end of Moses' white-water rafting trip, a new family adopted him. Noah's faithfulness saved his entire family from drowning. Jacob and Esau were brothers that spent most of their life competing and fighting. The sexual abuse of David's daughter by David's son is a case study for family dysfunction. Regardless of our family circumstances, rest assured there are examples of it in the Bible.

God calls Christians His family. Like our earthly families, some Christians are better family members than others are. To help us understand God's definition of family, He sent His Son to be part of an earthly family. The Christmas story models God's family plan. There is a mother and father tenderly loving a child, doing anything to protect Him. The Christmas story offers examples of cousins supporting each other through difficult but thrilling circumstances and an elderly couple celebrating the birth of a son they thought they would never have. There are also examples of the extended family of God that includes shepherds, a priest, a priestess, and Wise Men. Christmas is a time for fellowship with family.

Background Scripture

Read Ephesians 3:14-15. The Greek word used in this Scripture is *patria*. It means a group of families or a whole race (nation). What do you think this verse means?

_____

_____

The more common words for family used in the Bible mean circle of relatives, house, or abode. Our dictionary gives a broad definition of family, including a one-or two-parent house with children, circle of relatives, anyone who lives together in one household, and people committed to each other or bonded together in some way. In other words, no one need be without family.

Because I didn't want my children to ever feel like they have no family, I always told them that family is whom they are with at the time. I have a friend who lost the last three members of her biological family in one year. Brokenly, she said, "I have no family left." Yet, as she spoke, I noticed she was surrounded by a circle of friends, intent on taking care of her. They call her, take her out, take her to the doctor, and help with business affairs. She may not have relatives, but she is not without family.

Read Luke 12:52-53. Unfortunately, families are not always like Jesus' earthly family. The fact that there are so many dysfunctional families should come as no surprise. What does Jesus warn us could happen with earthly families?

_____

_____

Read Psalm 33:18-20. As a parent, I watched my children carefully, feeding and protecting them. They are now adults, yet I continue to have unfailing love for them. Describe the promise in this verse.

_____

_____

Read Jeremiah 20:11. My children used to perform in musical events. When nervous, they looked over, found my eyes, and drew the courage to proceed. Describe the safety we have in being part of God's family.

_____

_____

Fellowship With Family

White haired, tall, and lean, Bob Ivey greeted everyone with a smile and a hug. He loved God, his church, family, golf, and the Gators. In his youth, he played for the University of Florida Fighting Gators. I first became friends with Bob while coordinating a summer children's program that needed chaperones every Tuesday and Thursday. It should be no surprise that most people in the church were avoiding me. Knowing Bob used to coach football for youth, I asked, "Will you help chaperone this summer?"

One word was all he said. "Yes."

Stunned because I didn't have to beg, I asked, "How many days can you help?"

"How many do you need?"

"Actually, I need chaperones for every Tuesday and Thursday all summer."

"OK," he said. Was I hearing correctly? I resisted the urge to ask if he was joking. Faithful Bob attended every event that summer, with children always fighting to be included in his group. Bob became my hero and role model for who I wanted to be when I grew up.

Bob's fifty-five year romance with his wife Virginia was obvious to anyone that watched. When Virginia got sick, Bob carefully and lovingly tended her. He continually asked for prayer.

When she went home to be with the Lord, instead of groaning, he celebrated her eternal life. "I was so blessed to have been married to Virginia for fifty-five years," he told anyone who would listen.

I worried about Bob after Virginia died. His children were grown and I thought he was alone. "How are you?" I asked continually.

He always smiled at that question. "God has called me to continue living on earth. I'm just happy to still be here." Silly me. I shouldn't have worried. Bob saw everyone as family or potential family and was never alone.

Bob carried a business card with him and gave it to people as he told them about the love of God.

"The card helps me witness and gives people a way to get in touch with me," he would say. "See the picture of the rose? Virginia loved roses. I use it to tell people how beautiful a Christian marriage can be."

Bob knew no strangers and talked to everyone he met. "God says I'm supposed to tell people about Jesus, so I do." His business card also had a picture of a cross and praying hands. "I use the cross to tell people about Jesus, and the praying hands to tell them about the prayer ministry at church. Then, I invite them to church."

In the home where Bob lived with Virginia for forty years, her colorful roses blossomed year after year in their front yard. Eventually, the time came for Bob to move to a place easier for him to manage. Was this going to be hard for Bob? Again, I shouldn't have worried. Bob knew how to "let go and let God" and faced this change with the same positive attitude he faced everything else.

First, he asked for prayer. Then, he made sure Virginia's roses would continue living by giving them away. Since he moved to a smaller place, he took inventory of his belongings and kept only the essentials. He even found a way to get a recliner chair that he always wanted. Bob moved proudly, delighted with his digs.

"I love where I live and like to be around people. I enjoy having my meals prepared for me again." One of the definitions of family is people who live under one roof. Bob found a new family.

Bob loved his church family. His ministry was helping to coordinate the church's prayer ministry. For several years, I had the privilege of being in a monthly prayer group with him. He responded to my needs like a faithful family member, praying for my family, health, business, career, and ministries. He's even prayed for this book. I have prayed for his golf game.

Bob enjoyed the fellowship of his church family. He attended and ministered during all of the Christmas celebrations. I noticed him at the dress rehearsal for our church's Singing Christmas Tree. He was just there to help. On opening night of the Singing Christmas Tree, he helped to feed our guests, the city's homeless.

Bob knew who his Heavenly Father was and understood that his body was his Father's temple. He took care of his body the same way he would take care of any family member's home. "God wants me to take care of my body." Because he took care of God's temple, he was able to serve God faithfully. He faced the aging process with the courage of a warrior fighting in battle. For example, Bob's knee started giving him some difficulties. First, he asked for prayer. Without hesitation, he had a knee replacement. He went through the painful physical therapy without complaint and was back on the golf course in just a few weeks.

Bob loved Christmas. "Christmas is for families. I love the Christmas season because it allows me to reconnect with family members I haven't seen during the year. Christmas strengthens our family bonds. I spend Christmas with my church, children, and grandchildren."

"What was your favorite Christmas gift?" I asked.

He had no trouble answering. With tears in his eyes he said, "My favorite gift was a gratitude letter from a friend I helped. This letter contains my favorite Scripture and hangs in my new home."

In case you are wondering, Bob's favorite Scripture was also on the card he gave out as he told people about Jesus. Proverbs 3:6 describes the life of Bob Ivey.

"In all thy ways acknowledge Him, and He shall direct thy paths."

—Proverbs 3:6 KJV

Dedicated to the Memory of Bob Ivey - 2005

Application (5-10 Minutes)

Making It Personal

Write your favorite Scripture.

_____

_____

How can or do you share your favorite Scripture with the world?

_____

_____

Which part of the family fellowship of Christmas do you enjoy the most?

_____

_____

How can or do you use Christmas to strengthen the family bonds:
- In your home?

_____

_____

- In your church?

_____

_____

- In your world?

_____

_____

How well do you take care of the Holy Spirit's home, your body? How can you do better today?

_____

_____

Praying Continuously (1 Thessalonians 5:17)

- Take some time today for the purpose of fellowship with family.
  - Suggestions: Play a game. Go out to dinner. Make a phone call. Read to someone. Go to a party.
  - Praise God for your family as you do these things.
- Every time you see a family member, whisper a quick prayer of thanks.
- Stop and pray for any family problems.

Ending The Day

- Did you take care of the home of the Holy Spirit today? If not, confess and ask forgiveness.
- Were you a good family member today? If not, confess and ask forgiveness.
- Praise God for your family.
- Tell Him your concerns about your family.
- Praise God for letting you be a part of His family.

Romance at Christmas

Meditation (3-5 Minutes)

Begin by being still before God. Meditate on the words "Love the Lord your God with all your heart and with all your soul and with all your mind and with all your strength. The second is this: Love your neighbor as yourself. There is no commandment greater than these." (Mark 12:30-31 NIV)

- Be still and know He is God.
- Let your mind love God.
    - Surrender your doubts and questions.
    - Seek His knowledge for your purpose this Christmas.
    - Let your heart love God.
- Feel your emotions.
    - Give God any past hurt.
    - Feel His healing power.
    - Let the joy of the Lord enter your heart.
    - Seek understanding for the meaning of Christmas.
- Let your soul love God.
    - Worship Him in His mightiness.
    - Surrender other gods before him.
    - Ponder the wonder of spending an eternity worshiping Him.
    - Seek His wisdom for your actions this Christmas.
- Let your strength love God.
    - Surrender your exhaustion.
    - Ponder the wonder of your body being His temple.
    - Seek a way to use your spiritual gifts for Christ this Christmas.

- Love your neighbors.
  - Surrender fears about fulfilling His commission to tell the world about Christ.
  - Surrender selfishness.
  - Let yourself "disappear" as Christ takes over your spirit.
  - Seek a way to love your neighbors this Christmas.
- Listen to the voice of God.

Prayer (5-10 Minutes)

Appendix A: Requests of the Christ Child

- Ask God to speak to you during this devotional time.
- Pray for:
  - An eager mind this Christmas.
  - A healthy heart.
  - A pure soul.
  - A willing body.
  - Your neighbors to experience Christ at Christmas.
- List any needs in Appendix A.
- Ask for knowledge of His will for you this Christmas and the power to carry it out.
- Ask the Holy Spirit to interpret the scriptures you are about to read.

Appendix B: Gifts from the Christ Child

- Thank God:
  - For loving us.
  - For the privilege of loving him.
  - For the romances in your life:
    - With Him.
    - With your spouse or significant other.
- List your romances, past or present, in Appendix B.

Appendix C: Gifts to the Christ Child

- Offer God:
  - The love of your mind, heart, soul, and strength.
  - Your love for His children.
  - Your romances.
- Appendix C: Pray and update.

Appendix D: Celebrations for the Christ Child

- Look at Appendix D and make sure you have planned time for romance this Christmas.
- Fill in your "To Do" list, praying about each action.

Bible Study (10-15 Minutes)

When we think of a romance, we automatically think of the search for the person God planned as our spouse. Our society romanticizes dating, but let's be realistic. Dating is difficult at best. Yes, there is the thrill of the chase, but unfortunately, it doesn't stop there. There is insecurity as you wonder what someone thinks about you. As a female, I have to insert the pressure of what to wear. Fear of hurt from rejection reigns in the dating game. How about the uncertainty of deciding how much to reveal as dating couples get to know each other? Also, one must never underestimate the stress of intimate temptations.

I always told my children that the purpose of dating was mate elimination. I suggested they date someone until they are certain this individual is not God's choice for their life. Once the person is "off the list," move on immediately. I wanted them to leave more time for God's choice for their lives. I reminded them that the Bible says being single is more blessed than being married.

I am not in favor of long engagements for Christians. There is too much physical temptation that could have a lasting impact on life and marriage. My other advice to my children was the following: "Once someone has been 'on the list' for an acceptable amount of time and you are sure they are the right one, do not wait for the 'perfect time.' Marry them immediately once you are sure that the union is God's will. The circumstances will work themselves out."

Background Scripture

Romance is not just for dating. Song of Solomon is a book about romance. Solomon is demonstrating how married couples should respond to one another. The deeper meaning of the book describes the nature of our romance with God. Whether you are single or married, this devotion is for you.

Read Song of Solomon 1:4. Describe a time when you have felt that way about someone else.

_____

_____

Describe a time when you have felt that way about God.

_____

_____

Read Song of Solomon 4:10. How does God plan for us to feel about our spouses?

_____

_____

"But wait," you cry. "You don't understand what I have to put up with. You should hear what he or she has done." Read Matthew 6:14-15. What is the secret to living with the imperfections of another?

_____

_____

Are you perfect in the romances in your life? Read Numbers 5:6-7. Who are we unfaithful to when we hurt other people? What are we supposed to do when we hurt others?

_____

_____

Read John the Baptist's words in John 3:28-30. Who is our bridegroom? How do we feel when we hear his voice?

_____

_____

Many reading this are single. Read 1 Corinthians 7:23-24. Some readers know God has called them to remain single for their entire lives. What is the blessing of this calling?

_____

_____

Some singles reading this long to be married. Read Proverbs 4:11-12. What does God promise? Apply this Scripture to your longings.

_____

_____

In our Christmas romances, we see several different romantic relationships. We see a picture of a long time marriage in the story of Zechariah and Elizabeth. We also see their personal romance with God. Then there's Mary and Joseph's courtship and their eventual marriage. They loved each other but put their love for God above all else. As far as we know, God called John the Baptist to be single. He had a specific purpose and didn't need distractions. John the Baptist understood romance and was called the bridegroom by Jesus.

Read Luke 2:36-38. What was Anna's romantic status? She was a widow. Do you think she was without romance?

_____

_____

A Christmas Proposal

Jack and Millie Humphries are part of our church family. They are very much in love and have been married for fifty-two years. Jack says, "My breath still catches when I see Millie walk in the room." One can certainly see why. Millie is beautiful. Jack and Millie are both teachers. Millie teaches private piano lessons and Jack teaches physics at a university. Their romance has included serving the Lord together for their entire marriage. Jack and Millie teach a very large Sunday School Class in our church. They also sing in the choir together.

My favorite story about Jack involves a disruption in the worship service. One Sunday, an inebriated man entered late to the service. He was filthy, his odor following him, as he walked up the aisle, talking loudly to everyone. He sat in the front and continued talking. The deacon telling the story said, "I wondered what to do. A couple of us got together to suggest options. While we were discussing it, Jack got out of his seat and sat with the man. He put his arm around him and pulled him close. The man laid his head on Jack's shoulder, went to sleep, and slept through the rest of the service. Jack's love was a witness to me. I will never forget the lesson I learned as he took action while the rest of us were still talking."

I asked Millie about her favorite Christmas gift. "That's an easy question," she said as she held up her hand. "The best gift I ever received was my engagement ring. Jack and I started dating in high school. He had gone off to college and we were separated for a semester. I missed him so much. On Christmas Eve, he came to my house and asked me to marry him. I quickly said yes. We were married a couple of years later."

Jack and Millie still treasure each other. They look at each other with love in their eyes. They continue to be tender with one another. Millie told me, "Everyday with Jack is like Christmas."

Christmas Romance In The Touchton Family

The Christmas Season is a special time for romance in the Touchton family. In fact, December 13th is our special romantic day. Bob and I met at the Jacksonville Fair the last week in October of 1967. We were in the 10th grade and became "enemies at first sight."

I was at the fair with my parents and girlfriend, Sandra. Bob and his friend Barry had worked at the fair to earn free ride tickets. Barry and Sandra recognized each other and, without a backwards glance, they ran off together.

Bobby and I stared at each other. My first impression of him was that he was too thin and had hair too long. I did notice his lovely blue eyes. His first words didn't bode well for our evening. "You won't be using any of my free tickets."

"I wouldn't accept them if you offered to pay me," I retorted as we walked in stony silence. I thought about leaving but my parents had strict rules about females walking around fair grounds alone. I was stuck with Bobby for the evening. *Sandra was going to pay*. We spent the next two hours riding together. It was a dangerous and acrobatic act to ride a Ferris Wheel without touching.

10:00 P.M. was the meeting time with my parents. Barry and Sandra showed up on time, arm in arm. Bobby and I arrived glaring. Daddy was carrying a gold fish. "I won it by swallowing a live gold fish," he insisted.

Bobby stared with those intense blue eyes. *"No you didn't.* No one would let you do that," he communicated in typical fifteen-year-old fashion. Daddy met his gaze and stuck to his story.

Driving home, Daddy remarked, "That young man was rude." He got no argument from me.

Bobby and I went to the same high school. To our disgust, we had Band and English together. Since we spent the rest of the year sniping at each other daily, the entire band knew of our animosity.

Early December of the following year, Sandra had her sixteenth birthday party. Having just broken up with someone, I went alone. Being a typical geek, Bobby had no date. Since we were the only two singles at this event, we took some teasing about being together and neither of us appreciated it. Tensions grew as the night progressed and things finally came to head when Bobby said, "Did you plan this just to get a date with me?"

When I've had enough, most remember my reaction and this night was no exception. I roughly grabbed his arm and dragged him into the hall. I could hardly breathe. Furious, I blasted him with a speech that lasted for the next several minutes. "You've been *rude* to me for an entire year and I've done *nothing* to deserve this treatment. *No one* else treats me this way and you're going to stop *right now*. You *dared* to suggest I set this evening up to be with you. *Think about what you're saying.* Do you really think I would go out of my way to set up a date with you? If you've ever had a girlfriend, I don't know about it. I'm a majorette, popular, and have had boyfriends since I was twelve." I proceeded to give him a list of everyone I'd gone steady with over the years. I finished my grand speech with, "You only wish that you could be so blessed as to have a date with me." OK, I admit to laying it on thick, but I was angry. The truth of my dating experience was that going steady meant hanging out at school and occasionally having boys visit my chaperoned home. I'd only been formally dating since I had turned sixteen the August before. I was, however, comfortable with the opposite sex and meant what I said about my lack of interest in dating him.

Bobby was stunned. We stood there staring silently at each other. He then looked directly at me with those beautiful blue eyes and said, "You're right. I've been a jerk and I'm sorry."

It was my turn to be stunned. Everything changed between us at that moment. I saw strength of character and the ability to take responsibility for actions. I think I began falling in love with him standing in that hall. "Apology accepted. I probably could have acted a little better myself. Can we be friends?" People were staring as we walked out of the hall smiling.

Later that evening, I found out Bobby and Barry didn't believe in Christ and I grew concerned. Everyone knew Bobby and Barry were electronic geniuses. They even had their own radio show. "How about coming to our church tomorrow night?" I invited. "We're doing a Christmas musical and have no one to record it for us." Technically, this statement was true since there was no one to record it. The problem was that our Minister of Music didn't intend to record the program.

They agreed to come. Frantically, I called our Minister of Music and confessed. "They're not Christians. This was the only way I could think of to get them into church," I babbled. He laughed and cooperated with the scheme. When they arrived, he welcomed them. He even thanked them for their willingness to help.

After church, Bobby and Barry joined our youth group at my home. There Bobby and I discovered that we both enjoyed playing the piano and singing. I invited them to the youth hayride the next weekend. On December 13, 1968, Bobby asked me to go steady and gave me his ID bracelet. Our romance became the news item for our school. Not long after that, Bobby accepted Christ. That Christmas, he began the two great romances of his life.

In 1970, December 13th became special again. In my living room, Bobby got down on one knee and proposed. He'd already asked Daddy for my hand in marriage and by this time, my family loved him as much as I did. Daddy and I both said yes.

Bob and I are not the only Touchton's with a romantic Christmas story. Our son Chris and his wife Whitney also became engaged on December 13th.

Application (5-10 Minutes)

Making It Personal

- Who was the last person to whom you said, "I love you"?

_____

- Are you taking care of the romances in your life? How can you do better?
    - With God.

_____

_____

- With others.

_____

_____

Write a love letter to God, based on Song of Solomon, chapter 1.

_____

_____

_____

_____

- If you are single:
    - Thank God for the lack of "distractions" in your life.
    - How can you focus on Him more?

_____

_____

- Ask God to make your path straight if you are seeking a partner.
- Ask God if this is the life partner for you if you are dating.
- Ask God for wisdom for your future.
- If you are married:
    - Thank God for your spouse.

- What are his or her best qualities?

_____

_____

- How can you be a better partner this Christmas?

_____

_____

- How can you focus on God more?

_____

_____

- Ask God for wisdom for your future.

Praying Continuously (1 Thessalonians 5:17)

- Say the words, "I love you" aloud at least three times today:
    - To God.
    - To a friend.
    - To a family member.
- When you see people you know:
    - Think about what you enjoy about these people.
    - Thank God for them.

Ending The Day

- How was your romance with God?
    - Praise God for loving you.
    - If necessary, confess and ask forgiveness.
- How were the other romances in your life?
- Could you have been a better spouse, family member, or friend?
- If necessary, confess, ask forgiveness, and make amends tomorrow.

This devotion is dedicated to the sweetest, smartest, and sexiest geek I know. December 13 is the anniversary of "going steady" in 1968 and two years later, getting engaged. Happy December 13th Bob. I love you.

Christmas Ministers

Meditation (3-5 Minutes)

Begin by being still before God. Meditate on the words "Therefore I glory in Christ Jesus in my service to God." (Romans 15:17 NIV)

- Be still and know He is God.
- Think about God's glory.
    - Let yourself glory in the love of Jesus Christ.
    - Offer a willing spirit of service to our Glorious God.
    - Listen as He tells you where to serve this Christmas.
- Listen to the voice of God.

Prayer (5-10 Minutes)

Appendix A: Requests of the Christ Child

- Ask God to speak to you during this devotional time.
- Think about your own personal ministry.
    - Ask God for the time to serve Him this Christmas.
    - Pray for the wisdom to know where you should be serving this Christmas.
    - Ask God how you can utilize your spiritual gifts this Christmas.
- You have needs this Christmas. Write them in Appendix A.
- Ask God for people to minister to your needs.
- Ask for knowledge of His will for you this Christmas and the power to carry it out.
- Ask the Holy Spirit to interpret the scriptures you are about to read.

Appendix B: Gifts from the Christ Child

- Who ministers to you?
  - At home?
  - In church?
  - In the world?
  - Thank God for them.
  - Add them to Appendix B.
- Personal ministry:
  - Think of meaningful ways you were able to use your spiritual gifts on a previous Christmas.
  - Thank God for this privilege.
  - List them in Appendix B.

Appendix C: Gifts to the Christ Child

- Offer yourself to God as His minister.
- Ask God to show you how to better utilize your spiritual gifts as you give gifts this Christmas.
- Appendix C: Pray and update.

Appendix D: Celebration for the Christ Child

- Turn to Appendix D and update your "To Do" list.
- Are there ways you can minister at your celebrations? Add them to your "To Do" list.

Bible Study (10-15 Minutes)

We love God with our strength when we minister to others. Our spiritual gifts enable our ministries. One of our purposes is to serve God through these ministries. Throughout the Bible, we see people using spiritual gifts. Jesus demonstrates all of the spiritual gifts. The Christmas Story is an inspiring example of people ministering to others by using their Spiritual Gifts. Each of the ministers in our blessed story gives a different example of how we can minister to others.

Background Scripture

Read Romans 12:6-8. The seven spiritual gifts listed are:

1. Prophecy
2. Service
3. Teaching

4. Encouragement
5. Generosity
6. Leadership
7. Mercy

Zechariah

Read Luke 1:8-9. Zechariah actually had the title "Minister." When the famous angel Gabriel spoke to him, Zechariah was "serving as a priest before God." He was in the temple burning incense and praying for the people. Zechariah is an example of someone called to full-time Christian service. What gift or gifts do you think Zechariah demonstrated as he ministered to others?

_____

_____

Elizabeth

Read Luke 1:42-45. When Mary found out she was expecting, she headed straight to her cousin Elizabeth. They immediately worshiped together. Elizabeth's words ministered to Mary's soul. What gift or gifts do you think Elizabeth demonstrated as she ministered to Mary?

_____

_____

Friends

Read Luke 1:57-66. Elizabeth and Zechariah had good friends. Poor Zechariah left the temple mute. His friends could have judged him, but instead they shared the joy of Elizabeth's pregnancy. A joy shared is a joy multiplied. What gift or gifts do you think their friends demonstrated as they ministered to Elizabeth and Zechariah?

_____

_____

Mary

Read Luke 2:7. Our King was born into our world as a helpless baby. His mother had to feed Him, diaper Him, and sing Him to sleep. She did everything for Him. What gift or gifts do you think Mary demonstrated as she took care of Jesus?

_____

_____

Anna

Read Luke 2:36-38. Praying for people is another form of ministry. The prophetess, Anna spent her life in prayer and worship. She heard the voice of God and recognized Christ. What gift or gifts do you think Anna demonstrated as she told others about Christ?

_____

_____

Wise Men

Read Matthew 2:11. The Wise Men opened their treasures and gave the Holy Family valuable gifts. While we do not know for sure, it seems likely the Holy Family sold those gifts to finance the difficult days that lay ahead. How do you imagine they were used?

_____

_____

Read Matthew 2:12. God also used the Wise Men to protect Jesus. He warned them in a dream. They listened to His words. The Wise Men ministered to this young family by avoiding Herod and, thus, protecting them. They were willing to disobey Herod and risk their lives to protect Jesus. What gift or gifts do you think the Wise Men demonstrated in their part of the Christmas Story?

_____

_____

Joseph

Read Matthew 2:13-15. A confused Joseph listened to and obeyed the angel and married Mary. We see him taking care of his family the night Jesus was born. Joseph protected his family again when Herod was killing male children. God calls people to protect. Many risked their lives to protect Jesus' disciples. Paul Revere warned us that "The British Are Coming." People ministered in Germany by hiding Jews and in this country by hiding slaves. What gift or gifts do you think it takes to protect others?

_____

_____

Application (5-10 Minutes)

Making It Personal

What ministries are you involved in this Christmas?

_____

_____

Using the list from Romans 12:6-8, what are your spiritual gifts?

_____

_____

How are you exercising your spiritual gifts this Christmas?

_____

_____

Jesus demonstrated each of the spiritual gifts. God calls us to be like Him. Think of one way you can demonstrate each of the spiritual gifts during the Christmas season.

Mercy: Are there people around you who need your love, understanding, and/or forgiveness? How can you offer comfort and ease fear and doubt?

_____

_____

Encouragement: Are there words of encouragement you can offer to the world around you?

_____

_____

Service: How can you help meet the personal needs of the people around you?

_____

_____

Generosity: How can you be generous with your money? Can you give to help meet the material needs of those less fortunate than yourself?

_____

_____

Prophecy: How can you point people to God?

_____

_____

Leadership: Could you ease the Christmas pressure by providing leadership as people coordinate Christmas events?

_____

_____

Teaching: Can you tell someone the Christmas Story?

_____

_____

Praying Continuously (1 Thessalonians 5:17)

- Spiritual Gifts
  - Ask God how you can demonstrate at least one of the spiritual gifts today.
  - Obediently follow His direction.
- Praise God each time someone ministers to you:
  - At work.
  - At home.
  - At church.
  - In the world.

Ending The Day

- Were you a minister today?
- Did you utilize your spiritual gifts today?
  - If yes, praise God for the opportunity to be His minister.
  - If no, confess and ask for forgiveness.
- Ask God to help you fully utilize your spiritual gifts.

The Singing Christmas Tree

Meditation (3-5 Minutes)

Begin by being still before God. Meditate on the words "I will praise thee, O LORD, with my whole heart; I will shew forth all thy marvelous works. I will be glad and rejoice in thee: I will sing praise to thy name, O thou most High." (Psalm 9:1-2 KJV)

- Be still and know He is God.
- Praise Him with all your heart.
- Tell Him of His marvelous works and wonders.
- Be glad and rejoice in Him.
- Sing praise to His name.
- Listen to the voice of God.

Prayer (5-10 Minutes)

Appendix A: Requests of the Christ Child

- Ask God to speak to you during this devotional time.
- In Appendix A, ask God to send you music this Christmas.
- Ask God to help you notice His joyful singing over you.
- Appendix A: Pray and update.

Appendix B: Gifts from the Christ Child

- Thank God for music.
- Praise Him for the many ways we are able to use music to serve Him.

- Turn to Appendix B and list the ways music has blessed your life at Christmas.
- Ask for knowledge of His will for you this Christmas and the power to carry it out.
- Ask the Holy Spirit to interpret the scriptures you are about to read.

Appendix C: Gifts to the Christ Child

- In Appendix C, offer your talents to the Christ Child.
- Sing your own praise to Him.
- Appendix C: Pray and update.

Appendix D: Celebration for the Christ Child

- Turn to Appendix D. Thank God for the celebrations that involve music. Is there a way to add music to your Christmas celebrations?
- Pray and update your "To Do" list.

Bible Study (10-15 Minutes)

There is music throughout the Bible. David sings as he watches sheep on a hill. Angels sing as they announce the birth of Jesus. The disciples sang in prison. Mary and Elizabeth had pockets full of joy as they sang and rejoiced over their children. God, the creator of music, sings over us.

Background Scripture

Read Psalm 149:4. How does the Lord feel about you?

Read Zephaniah 3:17. The Lord is always with His children. He is mighty and saves us and takes great delight in us. Picture the Lord rejoicing over you. What does the Scripture say He does as He rejoices?

Read John 4:23-24. Our Father is seeking worshipers. How are we supposed to worship Him?

_____

_____

Read 1 Timothy 3:15. During Christmas, people who don't attend church any other time instinctively seek the Christmas music of the church. What does the Scripture say about the church?

_____

_____

Read Matthew 28:19-20. We call this Scripture "The Great Commission." At Christmas, how do we use music to make disciples?

_____

_____

Read Psalm 100. We shout for joy and worship the Lord with gladness. How are we supposed to come before Him?

_____

_____

Come Into His Presence With Singing

The 25th anniversary was finally here. The choir was giddy with anticipation. Southside Baptist Church in Jacksonville, Florida had spent days building and decorating a tree-shaped scaffolding inside the church, practiced diligently, dressed up as bright Christmas ornaments, and suffered the heat of the lights to offer a Singing Christmas Tree to their community. This year, their director, Rev. Eddie Lockamy gave the choir a list of everything they had ever sung and the choir voted for their favorites.

Anticipation was also building in the community and church. Over the years, the number of nights that Southside Baptist Church filled their sanctuary to overflowing has grown to five. Local restaurants and stores distribute free tickets that are gone in the first two weeks. Each night at 7:00 PM the celebration begins in darkness and the audience gasps as the tree lights up. At the end, the audience stands stunned and clapping, reluctant to leave.

The first night of the performance is for the homeless and prison community. The next three are for the community at large with church members coming the last night. While the choir is comprised mostly of church members, others from the community also join the singing. The tree usually has around seventy singers dressed as ornaments. Each year, a choir member is given the honor of being the angel at the top of the tree.

Rehearsals begin with a "Christmas in August" party where the music is introduced. Choir members wait with anticipation all year to see the unveiling of this year's Singing Christmas Tree selections. There is always a blend of the familiar and the new, as well as religious and secular. The choir tells the entire Christmas story, from the cradle to the empty tomb.

In many churches, the music department is the war department of the church with temperamental musicians fighting for key positions and solos. Not so in the Southside Baptist Church Choir. Rev. Eddie has a different vision for his choir. "Our choir members are worship leaders and servants. Each choir rehearsal is preparation for our church's worship service. I want our choir rehearsals themselves to be a worship service."

His choir rehearsals include prayer and devotions as he prepares the choir spiritually to be worship leaders. He lets the choir know what to be in prayer for. He told me, "I pray over the selections and the soloists. God often leads me to use unexpected selections and people." The choir supports his leadership, always believing "this year's selections are the best ever."

In thinking about the Singing Christmas Tree's importance to the community, I realize that it fulfills God's greatest commandment, to love Him with all of our heart, soul, mind, and strength, and to love our neighbors as ourselves (Luke 10:27).

Loving God With Our Soul

We are created for God's pleasure and He rejoices over us with singing. God constantly seeks worshipers that love Him with their entire souls. The Singing Christmas Tree is a Worship Service. The choir members worship while preparing it and the audience worships while hearing it. There is a time for everyone to sing Christmas carols during the service. Because the worship experience is centered on the Christmas Story, the Singing Christmas Tree congregation worships "in spirit and in truth."

Loving God With Our Hearts

The entire church pulls together to help the Singing Christmas Tree and has fun while they do it. Laughter can be heard all over the church as the large team sets up the tree made of scaffolding from floor to ceiling, in what serves as the choir loft the rest of the year. People cheerfully handle publicity, parking, and hospitality. Many fellowship with the homeless over a meal preceding the performance. As people work and play together preparing for the Singing Christmas Tree, they learn to love God with their hearts.

Loving God With Our Strength

"We are God's workmen, created for doing good works prepared by God" (Ephesians 2:10). We love God with our strength by ministering to the people around us. The Singing Christmas ministers to the Jacksonville community by sharing the Spirit of Christmas. People leaving on the last night said:

- "This is part of my Christmas every year. We look forward to it."
- "It would not be Christmas for us without the Singing Christmas Tree."
- "I went last night. It was so good that I came back tonight with my entire family."
- "It gets better every year. It is always different. They should take it to New York."

One woman cried all the way through the carol, "Mary, Did You Know?" She sobbed as she watched the video of the crucifixion scene. "This is wonderful. I have worshiped," she said.

The church ministers to prisoners and the homeless by feeding them, leading them in worship, and sending them home with gifts. A church member told me, "This year my calling was to the homeless. I sat and ate with them and talked about Jesus. A man said he had ruined his life through drinking. I shared how Jesus had turned my life around."

Many people have their individual ministries for the tree. Sandy is in charge of hair and makeup. She is famous for making "big hair" and stocks a room full of hot rollers and makeup called "The Big Hair Room." One would not dare light a match for fear the hair spray would ignite.

Dee and Sadie help with the "standing chart" for the tree. It is a complicated task. Some want to hide on the back of the tree and others want to be "center stage." Height and voices are considered.

Cindy and Barbara help prepare "No Room at the Inn," a display of nativity scenes on loan from various members of the church. There are sets of all types and sizes. The room hosts family heirlooms, sets made and played with by children, and some acquired during distant travels.

Bill prepares the soloists who are accompanied by Betty and Gwen. There are so many others involved in the Singing Christmas Tree. All of these faithful ministers carefully "complete the work God gave them to do." (John 17:4)

Loving God With Our Mind

We love God with our mind when we study the life of Christ and become disciples. The Singing Christmas Tree tells the entire story of the birth, life, death, and resurrection of Christ. People learn about the intricacies of this beautiful story as they study and sing the words of the selections. The audiences listen to the words and learn.

In addition to learning about the life of Christ, the preparation for the tree provides "singing lessons" for many of the choir members. Professional musicians coach the choir on the individual parts and the solos. The choir learns how to stand, breathe, and sing properly. The choir members "study to show themselves approved" with their music.

Loving Our Neighbors As Ourselves

There is no greater love for our neighbor than telling him or her about Jesus Christ. The Singing Christmas Tree tells the world about Christ. The number of people who attend humbles the church. This event has become so large that the church considered moving it to the Florida Theatre, a vintage downtown movie theatre repurposed into a performance hall. They reconsidered as they realized that attending the Singing Christmas Tree is the only time many ever go inside a church. Southside Baptist Church believes part of its mission is to host this in the church building. The performers gladly give their time on multiple nights so all can hear.

Many people come to know Christ through the tree. Counselors are ready to assist with questions and decisions. Some members in the church say their first exposure to the church was through the Singing Christmas Tree. Karen is the Chairperson for the evangelism committee. She sets up a hospitality area where people are encouraged to come for cookies and coffee, and to ask questions. She carefully coordinates each night. "My calling is not necessarily to put out cookies but it is for a higher purpose," she said.

The Singing Christmas Tree is dedicated to God and offered to the community. The individuals who sing on the tree are treasures. Millie has sung on the tree every one of the twenty-five years. "I would not miss it."

Tina tells me, "I love singing in the tree. The weekend before the tree, other church members and I help with a migrant worker children's camp. Then I get to be on the tree. I consider those two weekends my entire Christmas Season. My favorite night is the night the choir sings to the homeless."

Claude remarks, "The tree has two purposes for me. The first is my personal Christmas worship. Preparing for the tree helps me during the season. The second is that I get to help others worship."

"I love music," JoAnn comments, grinning. "I feel blessed to be part of a musical production. I have been a Christian for only five years and am 'on fire' to share Jesus' love. The Singing Christmas Tree shares the love of Jesus."

Faye loves singing on the night Southside feeds the homeless because they are so appreciative. "They clap, whistle, and cheer. I also enjoy practicing and fellowshipping with the choir members."

Kathy is fun to watch. She sings with all of her heart. She knows every word. "I love to praise God with music. Music is something that reaches everyone."

Cindy said, "I love music and I love Christmas. The Singing Christmas Tree combines my two favorite things, so it is a natural for me. I love being a part of something that shares the love of Christ with the community."

Phil is the Master of Ceremonies, soloist, and choir member. "I love doing this. I offered for us to do this for two weeks, but no one agreed with me." Phil's main concern is reaching people for Christ. On the last night, he walked over to the hospitality desk. "Did anyone find Christ tonight? I can always hope."

Application (5-10 Minutes)

Making It Personal

Is music a part of your Christmas season? Do you take advantage of the many beautiful Christmas productions available to you?

_____

_____

If you are a musician, are you using your abilities to tell the Christmas story?

_____

_____

This season, are you part of something that helps people love God with their entire heart, soul, mind, and strength, and love their neighbors as themselves?

_____

_____

Praying Continuously (1 Thessalonians 5:17)

- Ask God to send you at least one person with whom you can share some part of the Christmas Story:
    - Trust that God will answer your prayer.
    - Be alert.
    - Watch for the opportunity God will give.
    - Be courageous.
    - Grab the opportunity.
    - Share your love.
- Throughout your day, listen for the music around you.

Ending The Day

- Did you come before God with singing today?
- If not, do it now.
- Be still and enjoy Him singing over you.

Believe, Belong, Become

Meditation (3-5 Minutes)

Begin by being still before God. Meditate on the words "All this energy issues from Christ: God raised him from death and set him on a throne in deep heaven, in charge of running the universe, everything from galaxies to governments, no name and no power exempt from his rule. And not just for the time being, but forever. He is in charge of it all, has the final word on everything. At the center of all this, Christ rules the church. The church, you see, is not peripheral to the world; the world is peripheral to the church. The church is Christ's body, in which he speaks and acts, by which he fills everything with his presence." (Ephesians 1:20-23, The Message)

- Be still and know He is God.
- Let the energy from Jesus Christ fill your body.
- Praise His power. Nothing is exempt from His rule.
- Meditate about Christ's church. Read each sentence slowly and let the words sink in.
  - Christ rules the church.
  - The world is peripheral to the church and not the other way around.
  - The church is Christ's body in the world.
  - Christ speaks and acts in the church.
  - In Church, Christ fills everything with His presence.
  - Experience the wonder of being a part of Christ's church.
- Listen to the voice of God.

Prayer (5-10 Minutes)

Appendix A: Requests of the Christ Child

- Do you know that you belong with the family of God?
    - If yes, praise God for your church.
    - If no, ask God to help you find a church. Write the request in Appendix A.
    - If you are living on the "fringe" of a church, confess.
    - Ask God to show you what He wants you to do.
    - If you feel you haven't enough time, ask God for the time to belong.
    - Write your request in Appendix A.
- If your church is having difficulties, pray for your church and add the request to Appendix A.
    - Ask to see the situation with clear eyes.
    - Ask God to help you be part of the solution and not part of the problem.
- Ask for knowledge of His will for you this Christmas and the power to carry it out.
- Ask the Holy Spirit to interpret the scriptures you are about to read.

Appendix B: Gifts from the Christ Child

- List your church in Appendix B.
- Praise God for belonging to His family.
- Praise God for speaking through the church.
- Thank God individually for meaningful people in your church family and list their names in Appendix B.

Appendix C: Gifts to the Christ Child

- In Appendix C, offer God your service to the Family of God.
- Appendix C: Pray and update.

Appendix D: Celebration for the Christ Child

- Turn to Appendix D and update your "To Do" list.
- How many of your celebrations involve your church?

Bible Study (10-15 Minutes)

Christmas Eve worship services attract people all over the world. For some, this is their only church service for the entire year. Why, when Christmas is such a busy time, do people find their way inside a church? I believe it's because people instinctively know that church is where they belong. Jesus Christ is the cornerstone of the church and at Christmas, people long to be near such sweet truth. Christmas leads the world to seek Christ through the church.

The church offers a place to believe, belong, and become. The church helps us believe in Jesus Christ. We belong in a church. The church helps us to become the person God intends us to be. Christians desperately need to be with other Christians, particularly at Christmas.

Background Scripture

Believe

Read Mark 1:15. What are we supposed to do before we believe?

_____

_____

What do you think the good news is?

_____

_____

Read Mark 5:36. Believing is a command. What does the Scripture tell us?

_____

_____

Read Mark 16:16. What is the consequence of not believing?

_____

Read John 14:11. Sometimes it is hard to believe based on faith. What does Jesus offer as an alternative?

_____

Read Acts 15:11. What action brings salvation?

_____

What do you think the first Christmas has to do with salvation?

_____

_____

Belong

Read John 15:19. Where do we belong?

_____

_____

Read Ephesians 2:19-22. Once we believe, we are fellow citizens with God's people and members of God's household. Our temporary dwelling place is a difficult place to live and we need our communion with God and God's people to keep our vision of the Kingdom of God. The family of God gathers in His church. Who was the foundation? Who is the Chief Cornerstone?

_____

Read 1 Timothy 3:15. What is the church?

_____

Read John 4:23-24. How are Christians supposed to worship when they come together?

_____

Refer back to 1 Timothy 3:15. Where do we learn truth?

_____

Read Matthew 7:15-20. We have a church because Jesus came as a baby, died on a cross, and returned from the grave. Jesus himself instituted His church. Be warned. There are many false prophets. A true church has Jesus Christ as the cornerstone. How can we recognize truth?

_____

Read Ephesians 2:19b from the Living Bible. "You are members of God's very own family, citizens of God's country, and you belong in God's household with every other Christian." Where do we belong?

_____

Become

Read John 1:12-13. If we believe in Jesus' name, what is it our right to become?

_____

_____

Read 2 Peter 3:17-18. What are we supposed to be on guard against? How do you think the church helps with this?

_____

_____

How are we to grow? How do you think the church helps with this?

_____

_____

Read 1 Corinthians 9:19-23. Our commission is to tell others about Christ. What are we to become in order to lead people to Christ? What do you think this means?

_____

_____

Beloved Church

The many church families that call me one of their own bless my life. I have officially "belonged" to four churches and felt a part of many more. I grew up belonging to Murray Hill Baptist Church in Jacksonville, Florida, where many of my family still attend. The long upstairs halls where I loved to chase my friends and hear my echo still look much the same. The noble sanctuary with the colorful stained glass arched windows matches my wedding pictures. Many of the men who smiled at my childish antics still pass the offering plate today.

The people at Murray Hill are part of my extended family. They taught me to believe in Jesus Christ and helped me to become the woman I am. Mrs. Anderson helped me discover a talent for public speaking that I have used throughout my life and ministry. Mrs. Jarriel inspired a love for sharing Jesus Christ with others. Mrs. McGuffin taught me about being a godly wife and Mrs. Gunn taught me to laugh. Mr. Bagnal led me to Christ and Dr. Carl Howell baptized me. When I visit, I feel as though I'm home.

My college church was North Central Baptist Church in Gainesville, Florida. They made leaving home for the first time easier and helped me become an adult. In 1974, we moved to Pennsylvania where we "belonged" to Monroeville Baptist Church. This church helped me become a godly wife and mother. On a recent visit there, their marquee said, "Believe, Belong, and Become." The church was truly such a place for our family.

We have belonged to Southside Baptist Church for twenty years. They helped my son and daughter to believe in Christ. Southside developed their personal ministries and helped them to become the fine adults they are today. Vivian Goodwin's love for people helped me to become loving. Rev. Ron Henson offered an understanding of Luke 10:27 that became the cornerstone for God's ministry call in my life. Rev. Eddie Lockamy helped me become a true worshiper of God and Jim Gandy helped me become faithful to my church family. Dr. Wayne Stacy helped me believe that the church is the closest we can get to the Kingdom of God while still on planet earth.

There are other churches where I feel as though I belong. Uncle Bobby and Aunt Ka Ka's sweet church, Hart Haven Baptist, loves me as though I were her own. Aunt Ka Ka helped me become a pianist and some of my earliest recitals were held at their church. Hart Haven's confidence in me helped me find my place in ministry. First Baptist Church in Gainesville, Florida has adopted us and become our "middle of the week church" while Bob is pursuing a PhD in Robotics at the University of Florida. Their Tuesday night Bible Study has helped me become true to my calling.

One definition of belonging is to fit into a group naturally. When traveling across America, I visit churches of all sizes and denominations. The worship styles vary greatly but the message of love is mostly the same. Usually, I have an instant feeling of belonging because I am worshiping with Christians. A church of the living God is a place to belong. Belonging to a place that is the pillar and foundation of the truth is a privilege. Fill your pockets with Christmas this season by going to church.

Application (5-10 Minutes)

Making It Personal

Write a letter to God thanking Him for establishing the church. Tell Him what the church has meant to you. Praise Him for revealing truth to the church. If you have been unfaithful to His bride, confess. Ask how you can better serve Him in the church.

Praying Continuously (1 Thessalonians 5:17)

There are churches everywhere. Notice them. Look at the Christmas decorations surrounding them. When you see a church or hear a reference to a church, praise God for establishing His living church.

Ending The Day

- Do you love your church family?
- If yes, praise God for them.
- If no, ask God for help.

- If you have been participating in arguments and dissension in your church, confess and ask God to restore your vision for His church.
- If you do not have a regular place of worship, commit to your Father that you will begin the process of finding a church this Sunday.

I Need a Baby Jesus

Meditation (3-5 Minutes)

Begin by being still before God. Meditate on the words "Praise ye the LORD. Praise God in his sanctuary: praise him in the firmament of his power. Praise him for his mighty acts: praise him according to his excellent greatness. Praise him with the sound of the trumpet: praise him with the psaltery and harp. Praise him with the timbrel and dance: praise him with stringed instruments and organs. Praise him upon the loud cymbals: praise him upon the high sounding cymbals. Let every thing that hath breath praise the LORD. Praise ye the LORD." (Psalm 150 KJV)

- Be still and know He is God.
- Praise the Lord.
- Praise God in the sanctuary of your heart.
- Praise His mighty heavens.
- Praise Him for His surpassing greatness.
- Let everything that has breath, praise the Lord.
- Listen to the voice of God.

Prayer (5-10 Minutes)

Appendix A: Requests of the Christ Child

- Ask God to speak to you during this devotional time.
- For Christians, every personal encounter we have may be part of God's master plan to lead someone to Christ.
- Ask God for opportunities to show others Jesus today.

- Pray for the people in your life who do not know Christ and list them in Appendix A.
- Ask for knowledge of His will for you this Christmas and the power to carry it out.
- Ask the Holy Spirit to interpret the scriptures you are about to read.

Appendix B: Gifts from the Christ Child

- Is the Baby Jesus a part of your Christmas celebration?
  - If yes, praise Him.
  - If no, read the plan of salvation in the Bible Study below and invite Him into your life.
- In Appendix B, list the people who helped lead you to Christ.

Appendix C: Gifts to the Christ Child

- Turn to Appendix C and look at your gifts. Ask God to use your Christmas gifts as a witness for Him. Update carefully because Christmas is getting close. You don't want to leave anyone out.

Appendix D: Celebrations for the Christ Child

- Turn to Appendix D. Which of these celebrations could lead someone to Christ? Who can you invite to attend?
- Prayerfully update your "To Do" list.

Bible Study (10-15 Minutes)

Do you have the Baby Jesus? If so, are you sharing?

Background Scripture

Finding Baby Jesus is simple. Below is the plan of salvation. If you do not have the Baby Jesus this Christmas, I pray you will find Him and apply His truth to your life. If you do have the Baby Jesus, I pray you will share this plan with others.

Plan of Salvation

Read John 3:16. God loves us and has a plan for our lives. What is His desire for everyone?

_____

_____

Read Romans 3:23. Our own tendencies as humans separate us from God. On our own, we make mistakes that hurt others and ourselves. What does the Scripture say everyone has done?

_____

_____

Read Romans 5:8. What did Jesus do for us? Did He wait until we were worthy?

_____

_____

Read 1 Corinthians 15:3-6. How did Jesus demonstrate overcoming death and offering us eternal life?

_____

_____

Read John 14:6. God gave us a clear road map to Him. Who is Jesus and how do we find the Father?

_____

_____

Read John 1:12-13. If we believe in Him, what is our right?

_____

_____

Read Revelation 3:20. He is always standing at the door of our hearts and knocking. How do we let Him in?

_____

_____

A simple salvation prayer: Lord Jesus, I believe that you are the Son of God. I believe that You came to earth as a baby, died on the cross, and rose from the dead three days later. I am now willing that You should have all of me. I confess that I am a sinner and in need of salvation. I ask You to forgive me of my mistakes and become a part of my life. Thank You for loving me. Now help me to live for You.

I Need a Baby Jesus

I first met Sue when she was interviewing for a position at my company and instantly liked her. We worked side by side for several years, becoming close friends. She is fun, beautiful, and unbelievably loyal to those she loves.

Sue was not always the way she was when I met her. She had a difficult childhood. She grew up in a family that had struggles and addictions. As she became older, she began choosing the path that most of her family chose. This path took her on a long and difficult journey through the hells of addiction. Sue's captivity to alcohol followed the typical pattern. She found herself deep in the dark pit of addiction. Addicts have three choices: death, insanity, or recovery. She chose recovery. In her pain, she prayed a simple prayer, "Help." God heard and helped. Sue admitted she was powerless over alcohol and that her life was unmanageable. She got the help she needed and became sober. She took her recovery seriously and did what it took to continue, one day at a time. When I met her, she was leading a productive and full life.

While Sue was willing to ask God for help and to turn her life over to Him, she was not willing to believe in Jesus. Knowing she was not a Christian, I prayed for her daily. *Oh God, lead Sue to the truth. What should my involvement be? Please send others to help.*

God's answer was, "Wait for the right time." Being action-oriented, waiting is difficult for me. In September of 2000, our company hired a consultant to help with training. That consultant, Karen, happened to go to my church. Karen had just headed up our church's participation in the Billy Graham Crusade. Because of that campaign, her heart was prepared for evangelism. Sue had to work closely with Karen on the company project. She liked Karen and mentioned how special and grounded she seemed.

God whispered, "It's time."

"Sue, you are seeing Christ in Karen's life," was all I said. I thanked Karen for being a witness to Sue and Karen began praying for Sue. During the course of the next year, Sue and I had a few brief conversations about Christ. I let her set the pace. I shudder when I think of the damage pushing could have done. This was my lesson in patience and faith.

Sue had a couple of issues that needed prayer during this time. She asked our church to pray and they were faithful and followed up on her issues. God was faithful and miraculously answered Sue's prayers. One day, Sue came to me beaming, "Your church just called and asked me how my friend was. Wasn't that nice?"

On the morning of September 11, 2001, Sue and I were experiencing work pressures. People were flying in from all over the country for a business planning session. They were all due to arrive at noon. The CEO of our parent company was on a plane heading to Jacksonville. We saw no way to get everything done. Sue and I were frantic and snapping at each other. Sue looked at me and said, "We need to pray the Serenity Prayer and calm down." I completely agreed. She shut my office door and we held hands and prayed together: "God grant us the serenity to accept the things we cannot change, the courage to change the things we can, and the wisdom to know the difference."

As we finished praying, someone knocked. "You had better come watch the television." We arrived at the TV in time to see the second of the Twin Towers hit. We stood together stunned and crying. Our company gathered and prayed. People from all religions and beliefs participated in this prayer. Sue and I thought we were praying for "serenity, wisdom, and courage" to host a business planning session. How our perspective changed when the plane hit that building.

As CEO of the Jacksonville Subsidiary, I had my hands full. Because she worked directly with me, Sue had her hands full too. There were thirty-five people heading to Jacksonville on airplanes. Their families began frantically calling and we had no answers. Employees had relatives in New York and working in the Pentagon. One had a military husband who had shipped out the night before. All day, we had to deal with the terror of the people around us. We began the process of systematically finding our employees. Praise God they and their family members were all safe. Most of them spent the day grounded on an airplane.

In the middle of this mayhem, Sue came into my office weeping. "This is like Armageddon," she said.

My heart began pounding, a sure sign God wanted something from me. I stopped what I was doing. "Sue, Armageddon is going to be much worse than today." I briefly described it. "Are you ready for it?" I asked.

"I think so," was her hesitant answer.

"Sue, the Bible says you have to believe in Jesus Christ as your Lord and Savior for you to be ready."

She gasped and simply said, "I guess I'm not ready." We went back to work. As bad as things were that day, I knew the conversation with Sue was the most important thing that had happened to me. I wondered if I should say more but felt I should leave it alone.

For the next couple of months, Sue and I talked off and on about Christianity. Knowing she was a singer, I invited her to sing in our church's Singing Christmas Tree. To my astonishment and delight, Sue agreed. I prayed for her that Christmas. I hoped singing the words of the Christmas Story would lead her to Christ. I confess to being slightly impatient and discouraged with God's timing. Again, God gently reminded me to trust Him.

Sue loved singing on the tree. The people in the choir fell in love with her and surrounded her with the love of Christ. She was faithful to the choir and an asset to the performance.

Meanwhile, Karen had continued praying and was excited that Sue was singing in the choir. In January 2002, Karen helped start a "Seeker's Group" at our church. A Seeker's Group is for people seeking God in their life but who have questions. I invited Sue, who seemed interested but noncommittal. Several people from the church invited Sue, including Karen. "Are you asking people to call me?" Sue demanded.

I laughed. "You're going to have to blame that on God. You have made your own friends at Southside Baptist Church."

Our Singles Minister, John, introduced himself to Sue. Sue liked him and secretly named him "John the Baptist." One of the singles in our church, Jan, befriended Sue. John and Jan took Sue to lunch and maintained contact with her. Sue laughed and said, "I'm going to have to join the Seekers Group. Too many people have invited me." As she participated in the Seekers Group, her friendship with Karen blossomed. They occasionally met and talked privately. Karen offered prayer and support to Sue through this process.

The Seekers Group took on the challenge of Sue's bold questions and challenges. Sue is outspoken and a bit stubborn, yet they didn't judge her. Knowing Sue well, I knew this group had their hands full. Sue struggled with the news that Jesus was the only way to heaven. "I do not like the idea that a loving God has hell as an option. And how can Jesus be the only way to heaven?"

Finally Dave, a mature Christian, challenged her. He asked, "What is it that bothers you Sue? Does it bother you that it is true or does it bother you that we said it?" At first, Dave was afraid he'd been too firm. However, Sue has courage and appreciates honesty. Yet, she still had difficulty accepting the reality of hell from a loving God. Courageously, she continued to seek.

Sue knew God was working in her life because there were too many coincidences. At one point, I realized that Sue did not know the simple "how" of becoming a Christian and was making it too complicated. I shared with her that all she had to do was to confess her past, believe in Jesus' life, death, and resurrection, and ask Jesus into her life. We talked through the simple plan of salvation. I offered to pray with her when she was ready. "Thanks for the information," was all she said. I gave her a spiritual tract that had the plan of salvation in it. Sue was amused at how hard I was working not to push.

In April, I lost my job. Sue and I were devastated and cried together as we grieved giving up working together. I left on a journey dubbed Pocket Full of Quarters, which was a journey across America talking to people about God, listening to their spiritual stories, and writing those adventures on the website www.pocketfullofquarters.com. I felt bad leaving Sue in the middle of her "seeking," but God was in charge. Sue read the Pocket Full of Quarters website and she talked about the people I was meeting as if they were her friends. She passed my website address around to her friends. She found typing mistakes and offered to fix them.

While I was gone, church members continued to reach out to her. Her friendship with Karen deepened. Sue developed a deep respect for "John the Baptist" and continued going to the Seekers Group and asking questions. As I traveled, Sue gave updates on how God was working. She went in a public bathroom and someone had left a spiritual tract identical to the one I had given her. "Sue, you might as well give up and accept the truth. God is not going to let it rest." She laughed at my impatience.

God is so wonderful. During this process, Sue began dating the man who is now her husband. Rick is a Christian. Early in the dating relationship, Sue asked him, "Do you believe that Jesus Christ is your Lord and Savior?"

His simple answer was, "Absolutely." I came back to Jacksonville briefly to celebrate my 50th birthday. At the party Sue gave me a wonderful present. "When you finish Pocket Full of Quarters, I want to come to your house and ask Jesus into my life."

Again, I was impatient. "Let's do it now."

She smiled. "It will wait. I promise not to die before you get back." I considered cutting my trip short but Sue said, "And don't try coming home early."

I finished the journey. The day after I returned home, Sue came to my house. We sat on my back porch looking at the moon and the water. She brought her Bible. We walked through the plan of salvation and Sue marked the scriptures in her Bible. We looked up and saw a rainbow through the light of the moon. She read the Bible aloud, "For God so loved the world that he gave His only begotten Son." (John 3:16)

We came to places where I knew she struggled. Timidly I asked, "Do you believe what you've just read?"

She smiled and said, "Now I understand it. The Seekers Group explained it. Ray from work also explained one part to me." Sue and I held hands, laughed, and cried as she prayed, "Lord Jesus, come into my life."

The next Thanksgiving, Sue called to say she loved me. "This is my first Thanksgiving as a Christian. I'm grateful for Christ in my life." The next Christmas, Sue sang in "The Singing Christmas Tree" as a Christian. For the first time, she fully understood the words.

"How is this Christmas different for you?" I asked.

"When I went to put up my Christmas decorations, I realized I had no decorations of the Baby Jesus. I became frantic to get a Baby Jesus. I've found Baby Jesus in my life and needed a Baby Jesus for my Christmas decorations. Rick bought me a Nativity Scene that had a Baby Jesus. This Christmas, Baby Jesus is in my home and in my heart."

Application (5-10 Minutes)

Making It Personal

Are you a Christian? Have you turned your life over to Christ? If so, describe the experience.

_____

_____

If you are not a Christian, be courageous. Take the following challenge. Write the simple prayer, "Jesus, if you are real, make yourself abundantly clear to me." Sit back and watch.

_____

_____

If you are a Christian, be courageous. Take the following challenge. Write the simple prayer, "Jesus, remove anything in my life that is keeping me from having the best possible relationship with you." Sit back and watch.

_____

_____

Praying Continuously (1 Thessalonians 5:17)

As you go through the day, notice each encounter. Remind yourself that you may be part of the master plan for God working in someone's life and act accordingly. If there is an opportunity, big or small, to represent Christ, take it without fear or hesitation. Pray continuously for each person you meet.

Ending The Day

- Confess anything that came between you and Christ today.
- Did you share the love of Christ today? If not, repent and confess.
- Ask for more of the Baby Jesus this Christmas.

Keep in Step with the Spirit of Christmas

Meditation (3-5 Minutes)

Begin by being still before God. Meditate on the words "But let all those that put their trust in thee rejoice: let them ever shout for joy, because thou defendest them: let them also that love thy name be joyful in thee. For thou, LORD, wilt bless the righteous; with favour wilt thou compass him as with a shield." (Psalm 5:11-12 KJV)

- Be still and know He is God.
- Put your trust in God and allow yourself to rejoice.
- Shout for joy.
- Feel the wonder that He defends you.
- Feel God surrounding you with favor as with a shield.
- Listen to what He is saying to you.

Prayer (5-10 Minutes)

Appendix A: Requests of the Christ Child

- Ask God to speak to you during this devotional time.
- Ask God to help you keep in step with the Spirit of Christmas.
- In Appendix A, ask God for love, joy, peace, patience, kindness, goodness, faithfulness, gentleness, and self-control.

Appendix B: Gifts from the Christ Child

- In Appendix B, thank God for the Spirit of Christmas.

- Ask God for knowledge of His will for you this Christmas and the power to carry it out.
- Ask the Holy Spirit to interpret the scriptures you are about to read.

Appendix C: Gifts to the Christ Child

- In Appendix C, offer God your love, joy, peace, patience, kindness, goodness, faithfulness, gentleness, and self-control.
- Prayerfully update Appendix C. Resist the urge to rush out and impulse buy. Stick to your plan.

Appendix D: Celebration for the Christ Child

- Turn to Appendix D and update your "To Do" list. Resist the urge to add unnecessary tasks. Stick to the plan.

Bible Study (10-15 Minutes)

How is your Christmas Spirit this year? Are you keeping in step?

Background Scripture

Read Galatians 5:22-25. When we accept the love of Jesus Christ, our sinful nature is crucified and our gifts, if we accept them, are the Fruits of the Spirit. List the nine Fruits of the Spirit and beside each one, answer the question, "Do I exhibit them?"

_____

_____

_____

Read the Scripture carefully. Whose attributes do you think these nine characteristics describe?

_____

What do you think it means, "Against such things there is no law?"

_____

_____

When we accept Jesus Christ as our Lord, the Holy Spirit enters our hearts and lives. What do you think it means, "Since we live by the Spirit, let us keep in step with the Spirit?"

_____

_____

Love

The world is at war and pain and suffering is everywhere. Greed infiltrates the holiday season as people demand more. How can there be layoffs at Christmas? People are rude in the stores and in traffic and you wonder how the world can be so hateful, especially at Christmas.

Stop! "Keep in step with the Spirit." Choose love.

Read Galatians 5:13-15. God sums up the entire law in a single command. What is it? What will happen if we ignore this?

_____

_____

Joy

Memories from previous Christmases flood your mind as you think of people no longer here. Grief washes over you when you remember happier Christmases. Maybe you cannot go home for Christmas and self-pity threatens your Christmas spirit.

Stop! Keep in step with the Spirit. Choose Joy.

Read Psalm 98:4-6. Shout for joy to the Lord, all the earth. Spend your day bursting into jubilant songs.

Peace

People around you are tense and demanding. Children throw tantrums as they add requests to their gift list. Spouses complain about expenses as you worry about the same thing. Bosses want more from you and people around you don't seem satisfied with your best efforts. Hopelessness overwhelms you.

Stop! Keep in step with the Spirit. Choose Peace.

Read Isaiah 48:17-18. How do we find peace? What will it feel like?

_____

_____

Patience

Today is going to be busy because Christmas is almost here. You do last minute shopping and people break in front of the line. There are presents to wrap and no one wants to help. Family's coming to visit and no one helps clean. There's food to prepare but the lines at the grocery store are long. Work pressures and health concerns haven't stopped just because it is Christmas. Everyone is tense and you want to scream.

Stop! Keep in step with the Spirit. Choose Patience.

Read James 5:10-11. The Lord is full of compassion and mercy and willing to share. How do we manifest patience? Blessed are those who have _____.

Kindness

You remember your disappointments and hurts with past Christmases. Family dynamics are difficult during the holidays and you dread seeing certain people on Christmas Day. Family members are rude and you are tempted to give them what they deserve.

Stop! Keep in step with the Spirit. Choose Kindness.

Read Hosea 11:4. Do you see anyone who has a yoke on his or her neck? How can you lead others this Christmas?

_____

_____

Goodness

People are rushing and cashiers make mistakes. You just realized you have been undercharged but you are tired and the line is long. People at work make mistakes and you want to point to them. You make mistakes and want to hide them. Your boss invites you to go somewhere or do something you believe is immoral. You feel the pressure of keeping your boss happy.

Stop! Keep in step with the Spirit. Choose Goodness.

Read Romans 15:14. What are we to be full of? _____

Faithfulness

You were up late last night preparing and you know tonight won't be better. You're facing parties and shopping and exhaustion threatens your Christmas Spirit. Maybe you should stay home from that event or skip that task where people are depending on you.

Stop! Keep in step with the Spirit. Choose Faithfulness.

Read Psalm 108:4-5. How far does God's faithfulness reach?

_____

Gentleness

The unexpected will happen today. Someone will leave something undone and you don't have time for sloppiness. Someone may need an explanation that you've given before. People ignore your good advice and you feel like speaking sharply.

Stop! Keep in step with the Spirit. Choose Gentleness.

Read Galatians 6:1. How are we supposed to restore someone?

Self-Control

You look at your Christmas gifts and suddenly they seem small. You want to run to the store and buy more. You think of food that you could add to the Christmas menu. You have let your Christmas season become too complicated and want to take your frustrations out on your family. You are eating or drinking too much at celebrations.

Stop! Keep in step with the Spirit. Choose Self-Control.

Read Galatians 5:16. What happens if we live by the spirit?

A Fruitful Experience

The line was long and I was tempted to leave my gifts and go. It was December 18 so I persevered. As I got closer, I realized the cashier was new and making mistakes. *Great, she was calling the manager yet again. God give me patience.* Finally, it was my turn.

As the frazzled young woman began ringing up the purchases, I asked, "I saw a Christian Book Store somewhere. Do you know where it is?" She did and gave directions.

While checking me out, she made several mistakes. The scanner wouldn't work and finally she called the manager. "What now?" he growled.

I was tempted to sigh but since I had asked about a Christian Book Store, I suspected exhibiting patience and self-control was important. The cashier apologized and I responded with, "You're new. You'll get better."

The cashier took so long correcting her mistakes that people in the line were complaining loudly and glaring at both of us. She looked panicked and for some reason, I felt guilty. I quickly signed my receipt and bolted. As soon as I got to the door, it dawned on me something was wrong. The bill was $25 less than I expected. There were now ten people in line and my account was closed.

Normally, honesty is easy, but this time, I almost left. The voice of temptation whispered, "This was their mistake and going back will inconvenience everyone. Besides, one of those people in line might be a hit man."

That other quieter voice whispered, "Do the right thing." This time, I did sigh as I turned around.

"I don't think you charged me enough." Audible groans came from the line and I had visions of a riot breaking out.

"You are right," she said, going through my bag and scanning the receipt. Correcting the mistake took fully as long as everyone was dreading it would. The grumpy manager had to return and glared at both of us.

As the manager showed her what to do, she apologized. "I'm so sorry. Twenty-five dollars is a significant amount of money and this is taking a lot of your time. I can't believe you came back. Most people would've just left." Suddenly, I knew why God had put me in this circumstance.

"I'm a Christian. That's what we do. Besides," I joked, "if I'd left, God would've just continued speaking to me. Eventually, I'd have confessed and had to drive all the way back to this city just to pay you. Believe me, coming back now was easier. No amount of money is worth putting distance between God and me."

The cashier gasped. "You did ask me about a Christian Book Store earlier. Thank you for being honest." The people in the line heard the conversation. I don't know to whom God was speaking but I felt honored to be used. I was glad I had kept in step with the Spirit. In all honesty, if I hadn't asked about the Christian Book Store first, I'm not sure I would have been so patient. I left the store with the "Spirit of Christmas."

Application (5-10 Minutes)

Making It Personal

What is the Christmas Spirit? Do you have it?

_____

_____

Check yourself. How can you exhibit more:

Love? _____

Joy? _____

Peace? _____

Patience? _____

Kindness? _____

Goodness? _____

Faithfulness? _____

Gentleness? _____

Self-control? _____

Praying Continuously (1 Thessalonians 5:17)

Pick one of the "Fruits of the Spirit" to work on. Throughout the day, ask God to help you. As you go through your day, pay special attention to the fruit you picked. Choose to keep in step with the Spirit of Christmas through this Fruit.

Ending The Day

- Did you keep in step with the Spirit today? If not, confess and repent.
- Do you owe anyone an apology?
- Commit to allowing His leadership in your life tomorrow.

Christmas Rules

Meditation (3-5 Minutes)

Begin by being still before God. Meditate on the words "May the grace of the Lord Jesus Christ, and the love of God, and the fellowship of the Holy Spirit be with you all." (2 Corinthians 13:14 NIV)

- Be still and know He is God.
- Meditate on the grace of the Lord Jesus.
- Experience the love of God.
- Fellowship with the Holy Spirit.
- Listen to the Voice of God.

Prayer (5-10 Minutes)

Appendix A: Requests of the Christ Child

- Ask God to speak to you during this devotional time.
- Tell the Christ Child about what rules you this Christmas. In Appendix A, ask for relief.
- Tell Him about your busy schedule and ask for relief.
- In Appendix A, ask Him to rule your heart and your activities during the season.

Appendix B: Gifts from the Christ Child

- Praise God that He is God.
- Sing the words, "Glory to God in the Highest."

- In Appendix B, praise Him for sending Jesus to give us peace on earth.
- In Appendix B, praise Him for sending Jesus to give us good will to men.
- Ask for knowledge of His will for you this Christmas and the power to carry it out.
- Ask the Holy Spirit to interpret the scriptures you are about to read.

Appendix C: Gifts to the Christ Child

- In Appendix C, offer God your loyalty and your steadfast heart.
- In Appendix C, offer to be His peacemaker on earth and ambassador of good will.
- Update the rest of Appendix C, noting how many days left until Christmas.

Appendix D: Celebration for the Christ Child

- Turn to Appendix D and update your "To Do" list.
- Pray about what you have forgotten.
- Is there anything you can delegate to someone else?

Bible Study (10-15 Minutes)

This devotion is for those whose "To Do" list is longer than their "Time Left" list. It's for those good-hearted people who want to make Christmas good for everyone and are trying to be all things to all people, for those people trying hard to live life by the right rules and finding themselves overworked and overwhelmed. This study is also for those people who feel trapped into Christmas celebrations for which they have neither the heart nor the energy. If your Christmas season is going perfectly and you are thrilled with everything about it, you may either skip this devotion or merely review it so that you will have more compassion for all those who are still suffering.

What is ruling your life this Christmas? Perhaps it is "time." The newspaper says 50% of Americans have stopped putting up a Christmas tree with most giving time as the reason. Money, or the lack thereof, rules many homes at Christmas. Maybe worry, fear, family pressures, or a sense of duty is driving you forward.

Have you found yourself secretly wishing Christmas were over, or even wishing you could skip it entirely? You're not alone in those thoughts. While children's eyes light up at the thought of Christmas, many harried people anticipate it with some dread. Most don't skip Christmas, even if they fantasized about it. They take a deep breath and forge ahead, hoping this year will be different. They follow the rules established generations before them and find themselves resenting family pressures that dictate their Christmas activities.

For example, one family meets every year at 8:30 AM at Grandma's for a Christmas breakfast. Everyone dreads it. They wake their children early for gift giving and at 8:00 AM, they drag their family away from new toys and rush to the car. By mid-morning, everyone's exhausted and grumpy. At one point or another, every family member (including Grandma) has complained about this family tradition yet no one is willing to change it. If families aren't careful, what started out to be an enjoyable family tradition becomes a set of Christmas rules that governs the family and leaves our pockets empty regarding the Christmas spirit.

Background Scripture

Read Psalm 100:3. What does it say and how could it apply to the Christmas season?

_____

_____

In Luke 2:14, the angels tell us why Christ came and describe the Christmas Spirit. The King James translation says it most clearly: "Glory to God in the highest, and on earth peace, good will toward men." That is worth celebrating!

How did the birth of Jesus accomplish all of this?

_____

_____

Read Psalm 78:8. God speaks to us through our longings. Everyone longs for peace. When we allow the very season of peace to become frantic and nightmarish, what have we become?

_____

_____

What do you think it means to be loyal to God at Christmas?

_____

_____

What do you think it means to have a faithful or steadfast heart at Christmas?

_____

_____

Read Psalm 51:10. David's ancient prayer is relevant to what we all need for a holy and peaceful Christmas season. What two things is David asking for?

_____

_____

Top Ten Christmas Rules

There have been times in my life when I acted as if I thought I would make a decent god. I believed that everyone's well-being depended on me and worked hard to do my duty. I even believed that if everyone would do as I say, then their lives would work out fine. This character defect ran rampant at Christmas and most Christmases found me frustrated, disappointed, and full of self-pity.

Then I realized no one was paying attention to my many helpful suggestions. To my utter humiliation, I had to admit that it was all I could do just to take care of myself. Alas, I resigned from playing god and decided to let God be God. At Christmas, I turned to God and tried to get out of His way. My life and my Christmas seasons became peaceful. Family members seem to like me better. Ironically, I seem to have more influence on the Christmas season now than before.

Still, I must confess to occasionally thinking that I know how God ought to do things. I still want life on earth to be fair and sometimes grow indignant when it's not. If I were allowed to be god at Christmas, I would institute some Christmas Rules.

Cheryle's Top Ten Christmas Rules

1. Jesus: Everyone would know Jesus. He's awesome so it's a "no brainer" just to decide that everyone should know Him. I guess that means I would probably take away your free will and you would most likely react just as my family did.
2. Health: No one would be sick at Christmas. I wouldn't even allow colds (particularly when people are trying to sing in their church's Christmas presentation).
3. Home: Everyone could go home for Christmas if they wished to. Beloved and nice relatives in heaven could visit earth on Christmas. (Ornery ones could stay wherever they are.) Of course, we would have to get larger homes and cook more. Possibly, I could institute a correlating Christmas Rule that people visiting from heaven would eat no food and take up no room.
4. Equality: Gifts, food, and other resources would be distributed equally to everyone. *So much for free enterprise!*

5. Self Control: No one would overeat, get drunk, or participate in other damaging activities. Now you're thinking I've gone too far. In my world, I might do away with pie, cake, and certainly all alcohol.

6. Time: The days would be longer at Christmas. I talked to an exhausted woman who had just worked a twelve-hour day. She's against this rule.

7. Unity: Wars would stop. Everyone would get along. I'm not sure how to enforce this since the principle of this rule means I couldn't threaten them with a "nuclear bomb" if someone started a war.

8. Employment: Everyone would have jobs. No one would get laid off just before Christmas. Of course, if resources were distributed equally, why would we even have to work at all? OK, life might get a little boring.

9. Love: People would love each other. Of course, if I forced everyone to love, how would we recognize and appreciate the feeling?

10. Weather: The weather would be a warm 90 degrees. This is my fantasy and I love Florida!

You probably wouldn't like living by my rules. Some of them might be all right but many would prefer a White Christmas. I know from watching some of you eat that you would prefer a Christmas with pie.

My problem with these rules is I wouldn't stop there. I would also include some "Christmas Suggestions" with rewards for following them. I guess that would make me a god of works rather than a god of grace. This is sounding worse by the minute.

Cheryle's Top 10 Christmas Suggestions

1. Lighten Up: People would stop turning off all of my many singing, dancing, ringing, jingling, and snoring Christmas toys.

2. No Housework: I would have my housekeeper back. Of course, that means she would have to give up that exciting career she is enjoying so much. Oh, and I would probably have to stop writing these devotions to go back to work to pay for her.

3. Bubbles: Everyone would play with bubble toys. Surely, there is nothing wrong with that suggestion!

4. Schedules: People would be on time for Christmas dinner—the time I set. I don't eat between meals and I don't like getting ravenous before Christmas lunch.

5. Music: The family members would actually practice for the family Christmas recital. Is not there a Scripture that says "To whom much is given, much is expected"? (Luke 12:48 KJV) Since I gave them longer days, they would have time to practice.

6. Food: Aunt Ka Ka would always make her dressing on Christmas. Since she will one day go to heaven, I would have to make cooking a part of the work in heaven.

7. Cooking Lessons: Someone would teach me how to make whipped cream without its ending up on the ceiling and how to chop without cutting my finger on those sharp knives my brother gave me. I want the string beans to stop boiling over. In fact, I want the string beans to taste like my mother's and want to make dressing like Aunt Ka Ka. I seriously believe they leave out important "secret" ingredients when they share recipes. Of course, if I could make rules, I could decide to read their minds and find out the ingredients.

8. Gifts: The family would open presents one at a time. Why spend months buying and wrapping for it to be over in 20 minutes of paper flying and packages ripping?

9. Courtesy: People would remember the Christmas gift idea, phone number, address, etc. that I just gave them last week. Or, I could stop keeping all of those phone numbers and addresses in my PDA.

10. Grace: No one would ever get mad at me. That probably won't work since people are always getting mad at rule-makers.

Alas, my family will just continue to turn off my noisy Christmas toys and the world will continue to fight with one another until Jesus returns. People will get sick at Christmas and we will miss seeing people whom we love. You have heard my best efforts at playing god. It leaves much to be desired, so I think I'll just let God be God and use His three Christmas rules:

1. Glory to God.
2. Peace on Earth.
3. Good will to men.

Christmas Rules!

Application (5-10 Minutes)

Making It Personal

- Write your own set of 10 Christmas Rules. This is your fantasy, so write what you would do if you could make the rules for Christmas.

1. _____

2. _____

3. _____

4. _____
5. _____
6. _____
7. _____
8. _____
9. _____
10. _____

Now, write the potential negative side effects of your Christmas rules.

1. _____
2. _____
3. _____
4. _____
5. _____
6. _____
7. _____
8. _____
9. _____
10. _____

Praying Continuously (1 Thessalonians 5:17)

- As you go through your day:
    - Give glory to God in all that you do.
    - When you see any tension or conflict, pray and be a peacemaker.
    - Look for ways to generate good will between people.

Ending The Day

- Have you been trying to play god? Repent and confess.
- Did you think you knew what was best for people around you? Repent and confess.
- Did you give glory to God? If not, confess.
- Were you a peacemaker? If not, confess.
- Were you an ambassador of good will? If not, confess.
- Praise God for Christmas.

And the Light Became Flesh

Meditation (3-5 Minutes)

Begin by being still before God. Meditate on the words "For God so loved the world, that he gave his only begotten Son, that whosoever believeth in him should not perish, but have everlasting life. For God sent not his Son into the world to condemn the world; but that the world through him might be saved. He that believeth on him is not condemned: but he that believeth not is condemned already, because he hath not believed in the name of the only begotten Son of God. And this is the condemnation, that light is come into the world, and men loved darkness rather than light, because their deeds were evil. For every one that doeth evil hateth the light, neither cometh to the light, lest his deeds should be reproved. But he that doeth truth cometh to the light, that his deeds may be made manifest, that they are wrought in God." (John 3:16-21 KJV)

- Be still and know He is God.
- For God so loved the world, that He gave His only Son. Enjoy God's love.
- Whoever believes in Him will have eternal life. Anticipate an eternal life with God.
- God sent His son to save the world. Ponder the wonder of God's grace.
- Light has come into the world. Think about the Light of Christmas.
- Whoever lives by truth comes into the light. Are you living by truth?
- Are you living by the Light of Christmas?
- Listen to the voice of God.

Prayer (5-10 Minutes)

Appendix A: Requests of the Christ Child

- Ask God to speak to you during this devotional time.
- In Appendix A, ask God to help you walk in truth:
  - Throughout your day.
  - Throughout your life.
  - Through all eternity.
- Ask God to give you the light to notice and enjoy His world today.
- Update Appendix A with any requests and answers.

Appendix B: Gifts from the Christ Child

- In Appendix B, praise God for creating the world.
  - Praise Him for His beautiful creations.
  - Thank Him for turning on the lights so we could see.
  - Praise Him for the moon, stars, sun, heavens, flowers, and trees.
- In Appendix B, praise God for Christmas.
  - For the gift of His Son.
  - For the privilege of worshiping the Christ Child.
  - For fun at Christmas.
- Ask for knowledge of His will for you this Christmas and the power to carry it out.
- Ask the Holy Spirit to interpret the scriptures you are about to read.

Appendix C: Gifts to the Christ Child

- In Appendix C, offer God your awareness:
  - Of the beauty around you.
  - Of His truth.
  - Of His light, lighting your way.
- In Appendix C, offer God your willingness:
  - To be delighted with His gifts.
  - To enjoy the Spirit of Christmas.
  - To walk in truth.
  - To bask in His light.
- Update the rest of Appendix C. Do yourself a favor and make sure everything is wrapped.

Appendix D: Celebration for the Christ Child

- Turn to Appendix D and update your "To Do" list.
- Slow down and enjoy your final preparations and celebrations.

Bible Study (10-15 Minutes)

From the beginning, God offered light when He said "Let there be light." We look around in wonder at His creation and are grateful He created light first. Without light, the beauty would be a waste, as we wouldn't see the explosive colors of flowers, sunsets, and rainbows. Everywhere we look, God has given us things to see and enjoy through His light.

Instead of enjoying the light God offered, man rebelled. Our first rebellion was in the Garden of Eden. Adam and Eve just couldn't be happy with the gifts God gave them. The futile mutiny has continued throughout history. For our own good, God gave us the Ten Commandments but we were unwilling to follow them. He sent prophets, whom we ignored. Occasionally, He even spoke directly but we just kept right on being our own worst enemy.

God saw our darkness and once again said, "Let there be light." This time, the Light became flesh.

Background Scripture

Read Genesis 1:1-2 and describe the earth in the beginning. What was it like and how does that compare to life without Christ?

_____

_____

Read Genesis 1:3-5. The world was dark and God created light. What did He say about this light? How does God say, "Let there be light" in the lives of people?

_____

_____

Read Genesis 1:6-10. What did God create on the second day and what did He say about it?

_____

_____

Read Genesis 1:11-13. God created fruits and vegetables. He could have made everything the same but he gave us a wide variety from which to choose. He saw that it was good. Think about your favorite fruits and vegetables. Why do you suppose God went to the trouble to make them so different and interesting?

_____

_____

Read Genesis 1:14-19. God had already created light, yet even in light, He created variety. What was the purpose of the lights in the sky?

_____

_____

Read Genesis 1:20-25. God filled the water and the skies. He created birds and fish of all sizes, shapes, and colors. He filled the land with funny looking animals. What fun He must have had as He stretched the giraffe's neck and painted the zebra's stripes. He enjoyed His creations and who could blame him? How could you not enjoy watching monkeys play? Why do you think He created such variety?

_____

_____

Read Genesis 1:26-27. God made man in His image and let us rule over everything He made. This world was for us. What do you imagine the image of God is like? How are we like Him? What does that mean our potential is?

_____

_____

Read Genesis 1:28. God had already created a wonderland and yet, He did one more thing. What was that? Why do you think He did this?

_____

_____

You know the rest of the story. What kind of life did God plan for Adam and Eve in paradise? Did they live happily ever after?

_____

_____

Read Jeremiah 50:6. Adam and Eve are not the only ones who struggled. What happened?

_____

_____

Read John 1:14. We are God's creations, created in His image. God continually sent us light and we chose darkness. What did God finally do?

_____

_____

Read John 14:6-7. Who is Jesus?

_____

_____

Read John 10:10. Why did He come to earth?

_____

_____

The Aquarium

I dedicate this devotion to the memory of Steve, my late friend and mentor, who told me the following story many years ago. At the time, I was going through a "crisis of belief." I have retold it so many times I no longer know what parts are his and what parts are mine nor do I have any idea where the story originated. If anyone knows, please let me know.

A young boy dreamed of owning an aquarium. He visited fish stores and read books about fish. "I want an aquarium for Christmas," he announced.

"You're too young. This is too big a responsibility at your age," his parents argued.

"Please. I promise to take care of it," he begged repeatedly.

On Christmas morning, wonder of wonders, he received his aquarium along with the basic supplies. There was also a gift certificate to purchase fish and anything else he thought necessary. That morning, this little boy saw only this gift. His dream had come true.

Lovingly, he washed out the aquarium and found a table to put it on. He set up the equipment and turned on the light. How he loved looking at the light shimmering through the glass. He went to the store and looked at everything, choosing colored rocks, and trees and bushes of all sizes and colors. He bought houses, toys, and even a swing set.

He went home and set up his aquarium. Carefully he laid the rocks, using the different colors to create roads and trails. They looked good to him. He set up the house and put the swing set with the slide next to the house. He arranged the trees and bushes beautifully. All looked perfect for his fish. He filled the aquarium with water and made sure the temperature was perfect. He turned on the pump so the oxygen level would allow his fish to breathe. He loved everything about the world he had created.

Finally, the time came to buy the fish and he went back to the store. There were so many beautiful choices and he picked out the most interesting and colorful. Excitedly, he rushed home to put the fish in the aquarium. He sighed happily and sat back to watch.

He couldn't wait to see them swing on the swing. He imagined their joy as they slid down the slide. He looked forward to them traveling the roads and waited for them to take shelter and comfort in the beautiful homes. Surely, one of them would stop to notice the trees and bushes.

His dismay grew as he stared in shock at the fish swimming around in circles. They didn't enjoy the world he had made for them. They ignored the roads, swam past the swing set, and didn't notice the bushes and trees. None of the fish cared about the homes or sought their comfort.

Some of the fish even fought with each other. "Why are they fighting?" he cried. "Don't they know I'll take care of them and that there is plenty of room for all?" The little boy tried making the light brighter but it made no difference. They didn't even see the light.

As the little boy stared at his little fish world, tears rolling down his face, he said "Mommy, I wish I could be a fish just for a little while. I want to go inside the aquarium and teach them how to enjoy their world. I want to show them the roads and point out the beauty of the bushes and trees. I want to teach them the fun of playing on the swings and slides and offer the comfort and safety of the home. I want to light their way."

Sadly, this little boy didn't have the power to become a fish, but God had the power to enter our world as a baby destined to teach us how to live. On that first Christmas morning, the Light became flesh. This Christmas, turn on the lights.

Application (5-10 Minutes)

Making It Personal

Do you enjoy the beauty of God's world? List everything you can think of that's beautiful about Christmas. If you cannot think of anything, write a letter to God asking Him to help you see beauty.

_____

_____

_____

_____

Do you have fun in God's world? List everything you can think of that's fun about Christmas. If you cannot think of anything, write a letter to God asking Him to help you have fun.

_____

_____

_____

_____

Praying Continuously (1 Thessalonians 5:17)

Notice everything as you go through your day. When you step outside, look up and praise God for the sky. Look for the sun and moon and praise Him. Notice the flowers that bloom in the winter and thank God. If you pass a swing, take a moment and swing. If there is water near by, walk down by the shore and pray. If a child is playing, stop and watch. Discipline your thoughts today to notice everything wonderful.

Ending The Day

- Did you enjoy God's world today? If not, confess and seek His Light.
- Did you enjoy the season of Christmas today? If not, confess and seek His Light.
- Ask God to help you enjoy everything He has given you.

Peace in All Circumstances

Meditation (3-5 Minutes)

Begin by being still before God. Meditate on the words "To those who have been called, who are loved by God the Father and kept by Jesus Christ: Mercy, peace and love be yours in abundance." (Jude 1:2 NIV)

- Be still and know He is God.
- God calls us for His purpose. Think about your calling to God, the church, your family, your friends, and to the world.
- If we know Jesus, He keeps us. Let Him keep your problems, fears, hurts, dreams, and your Christmas Spirit.
- God offers mercy in abundance, even when we don't deserve it. Relax and enjoy it. If anyone has hurt you, offer him or her mercy, even if it is not deserved. Enjoy the relief.
- God offers peace in abundance regardless of circumstances. Enjoy God's peace this Christmas.
- God offers love in abundance. Bask in it.
- Listen to the voice of God.

Prayer (5-10 Minutes)

Appendix A: Requests of the Christ Child

- Ask God to speak to you during this devotional time.
- Are circumstances getting in the way of an abundant Christmas?

- Ask for God's will.
- Ask God how to pray.
- Write your prayer requests in Appendix A.
- Believe God will answer.
- Ask for knowledge of His will for you this Christmas and the power to carry it out.
- Ask the Holy Spirit to interpret the scriptures you are about to read.

Appendix B: Gifts from the Christ Child

- Thank God for His abundance and peace through all circumstances.
- Praise God for His mercy for us and others.
- Praise God for His plans for us in this life and the next.
- Praise God for loving us.
- Thank Him for answered prayer.
- In Appendix B, list abundance, peace, mercy, and love as blessings.

Appendix C: Gifts to the Christ Child

- In Appendix C, offer God your love this Christmas.
- Examine Appendix C carefully. Resist the urge to add last minute gifts. Joyfully, finish your shopping and wrapping.

Appendix D: Celebrations for the Christ Child

- Turn to Appendix D and study any last-minute preparations. Ask God to give you the energy to do what is necessary.
- Make sure there is a Christmas Eve worship service on your list.

Bible Study (10-15 Minutes)

Christmas Spirit depends on our relationship with God and not our personal situation. If we depend on Christ, we can have an abundant Christmas, regardless of circumstances. That's why it is called a peace beyond all understanding. Though our world can be frantically spinning like a top, through faith, we can relax into God's peace.

Background Scripture

Read Mark 11:22-25. Life can be uncertain, but God is always sure. When we face difficult circumstances, what does verse 22 tell us we must do first?

_____

_____

According to verse 23, what is the secret to answered prayers?

_____

_____

What is the promise in verse 24?

_____

_____

Read verse 25. To have effective prayers we must do one more thing. What is it?

_____

_____

The above verses, taken alone, can be confusing. Every word of the Scripture is true, but there is more to it. We all know godly people who have begged God for something, only to receive a no to their pleas. The answer to understanding this lies in studying how Jesus dealt with the difficult moments of his life. Jesus knew He was facing the cross. He was completely human and completely God. The human side of Him dreaded the pain and suffering of the cross. Read Luke 22:42-43. How did Jesus pray?

_____

_____

The disciples and followers of Jesus all faced and accepted difficult circumstances. Ephesians 6:18 tells us to pray in the _____ on all occasions with all kinds of prayers and requests. God's plan for us is an eternal one. When we pray "in the Spirit," our perspective becomes eternal. God's voice is clear and we can know His will as He leads us in how to pray. When we pray this way, Mark 11:22-25 becomes a reality.

Knowing we are in the Spirit doesn't mean our earthly circumstances are painless. The pain of the cross was real. The brutal ways in which most of the disciples died were real. Our pain on earth is real. Read 2 Corinthians 1:3-5. Where do we turn when our circumstances hurt? How does what we receive help others?

_____

_____

Read Philippians 4:7. We cannot avoid pain on earth but suffering is optional. Regardless of our circumstances, God gives us a blessing. What is it?

_____

_____

In closing, read Paul's encouraging words in Romans 1:8-10. How does Paul show deference to God through his prayers?

_____

_____

Difficult News At Christmas

"Bethany's going to need a kidney transplant," the doctor gently informed a distraught mother and daughter.

"But she's so young. She's only twenty. Surely there's another answer," Nancy, her mother, argued. Bethany had one kidney removed at birth. A progressive kidney disease was causing Bethany's remaining kidney to fail rapidly. While she had struggled with some health issues most of her life, this dire news came as a blow.

Bethany was a college student and enjoying normal campus life. She was a good student, a Christian, and her beautiful elf-like face glowed when she spoke. Although many young people stopped attending church when they left for college, not Bethany. "I get strength from church and my Christian friends. Of course I go to church," she said.

Nancy has been my best friend since high school. We often joke that Bethany is the perfect daughter. Bethany always laughs and says, "I'm far from perfect."

Bethany grew up in a Christian home. Her father, Barry, a full-time Christian minister, is on staff in a large church. Nancy plays violin in the church orchestra. Bethany has one sister, Allison, who loves her, and would gladly donate a kidney. My sense of fairness says this family has done everything right, so why were they facing a kidney transplant? It seemed particularly unfair to visit so many doctors at Christmas.

Concerned, I asked Bethany how Christmas was going. She looked surprised. "It's going great. I'll enjoy Christmas just as much as ever. I believe my doctors when they say that many people with a kidney transplant go on to have a family, career, and full lives. I trust God with my future. Doctors do make me nervous, but I go anyway. My main worry is Allison. I don't like it that my illness might cause her pain."

Bethany's mother, Nancy, depended on prayer to get them through this. After getting the news, she immediately asked her church to pray. While normally very independent, she allowed friends to help. "I can't go through this alone," she said. Nancy trusts God with Bethany's future. "I won't allow any thoughts except Bethany coming out of this healthy and whole. She will have a good life. There will be a kidney for Bethany." What some would call denial, others call faith.

The next year was difficult medically, with many trips back and forth to the doctor and hospitals, some of them emergencies. You aren't an official transplant candidate until your kidney function drops to a certain level. Waiting on that to happen is like being in the final stages of a difficult pregnancy, wondering when labor will start, and if the baby will be okay. Just before Christmas the following year, the doctors announced it was time.

Unfortunately, Allison's kidney wasn't a match. "I'm not worried," Nancy said. It was tempting to put Bethany on a list for a cadaver donor but Nancy stood firm. "Cadaver transplants are riskier and require higher doses of rejection drugs. We will find a live donor. Someone will be a match."

Anxiety overtook me. I knew people who had been on a transplant list for years. Yet, I should have trusted God more.

A friend of theirs fired e-mails to everyone he knew, asking for prayer and a kidney. Donna got one of those e-mails. Donna hadn't seen Bethany in 5 years and immediately called Nancy. "I'm the one. I want to be tested first. God has told me I'm going to be a match. No one else needs to get tested."

Again, I doubted. "What are the chances?" I warned Nancy. "Don't get your hopes up."

"Cheryle," Nancy scolded. "Don't cause me to doubt." She was right. I was feeling protective and didn't want her disappointed. I resolved from that moment forward, I was going to offer faith instead of doubt. Sure enough, Donna was a perfect match. The doctors wanted to schedule the surgery immediately, but Bethany put her foot down.

"I want to get through Christmas first. I'm also going to a Christian retreat in January with my friends." Nancy and I both fretted over this, but Bethany was insistent. "I'll be fine," she said calmly. "This will be the last chance I'll get to be with some of these friends because they're graduating. I need this retreat."

Bethany breezed through Christmas and enjoyed her retreat. She returned home spiritually centered and ready to face the future. She checked in the hospital, surrounded by family and friends. I counted over thirty people in the waiting room when she had her surgery. "Go home," she gently scolded. "I'll be fine." She hated worrying everyone. We stayed anyway.

As I write this 6 months after the transplant, Bethany and the donor are doing well. Donna never lost her sense of purpose or humor. When asked why she was willing to do this, she said, "When God tells you to do something, you'd better do it." "I'm blessed that God picked me." Donna is feeling great and is back at work.

After a transplant, life has all the ups and downs of riding a roller coaster. You take blood levels several times a week and hold your breath waiting for results. You go to routine checkups wondering if you will be hospitalized again. Twice Nancy has called and calmly said, "We're back on the roller coaster." Each time, the doctors solved the problem and Bethany came home from the hospital healthy again.

A Difficult Year

John had a difficult year. First, he lost his job. The loss was economy-related and not his fault, but he loved his job and his company. While grieving, he reminded everyone, "God is in charge of this situation." John held no grudges and wouldn't complain about his former employers. "The technology industry collapsed. They had no choice."

Not long after he lost his job, John had a routine physical. At the last minute, the doctor decided to order a prostate test. Surprisingly, they found an aggressive form of prostate cancer. This caught everyone by surprise since John had absolutely no symptoms. As John told us this terrible news with a trembling voice, he praised God. "God led those doctors to run that test. Normally, they don't test for this at my age."

Before this year, John had led a charmed life. "Until now, everything has gone right for me." He excelled in college and his soaring executive career generated a high income. He married and had the perfect family, a son and daughter. His wife takes care of the home and family while he goes off to work each day. They spend their late afternoons and evenings helping children with homework and attending sports practices. John is a Christian who has remained faithful to church. He teaches Sunday School and sings in his church choir. He's fun, a loyal friend, and easy to love.

The news of John's cancer shocked those of us who knew and loved him. It was hard to believe because he was so young and the picture of health. The doctors gravely told John, "This cancer had a rating of '7 out of 10' on the aggressiveness scale. The statistics for this are not in your favor."

John had the normal reaction of surprise and fear. "What about my wife and children?" he fretted. He turned to God and his friends, asking those of us closest to him to pray. He called us asking, "Would you please invoke the Jacksonville prayer warriors on my behalf?" Bob and I immediately went to our knees for John. That first night, we both cried as we held each other and prayed. We made a mental decision to go through this emotionally with him. God gave us a sense of peace as we realized that God led those doctors to find this cancer early and that He was taking care of John. As we prayed, God brought Mark 11:22-25 to our mind:

> 'Have faith in God,' Jesus answered. 'I tell you the truth, if anyone says to this mountain, 'Go, throw yourself into the sea,' and does not doubt in his heart but believes that what he says will happen, it will be done for him. Therefore I tell you, whatever you ask for in prayer, believe that you have received it, and it will be yours. And when you stand praying, if you hold anything against anyone, forgive him, so that your Father in heaven may forgive you your sins.' (NIV)

The morning after we got the news, I did two things. I made sure I was not holding any grudges against anyone. I didn't want my prayers on John's behalf blocked by my shortcomings. That was when I realized I was angry with John's former employer. I don't like it when people hurt my friends. I confessed and asked for healing. Gently, I felt my anger being replaced by love.

The second thing I did was to send out an e-mail request to the "prayer warriors" that John referenced. They immediately e-mailed their willingness to pray. Ray, also a friend to John, e-mailed me Mark 11:22-25 on John's behalf. God had now given that Scripture to both Ray and me. I knew God was leading us to pray for John's complete healing. I e-mailed this Scripture to John and told him what I was praying for.

John e-mailed back, "I am overcome with the outpouring and support from my Christian and non-Christian friends. My Lord is sustaining me. I am buoyed, and though I feel myself sinking sometimes, I raise myself up by praising Him. I am supported by a great church community that I now realize encompasses the entire United States. Christians catch on fire and spread themselves when others are hurting. I am being transformed even as I type this. My faith is being transformed. My being is being transformed. My relationship with my Lord is being transformed. How humble and grateful I have become."

Throughout the surgery and treatment for cancer, God ministered to John's spirit. Once, while waiting nervously to see a doctor, he looked up to see the father of his daughter's friend walking by. John knew the man was a doctor but hadn't seen him in years. "Why are you here?" the doctor asked. John explained what he was waiting on. Without asking, this doctor grabbed both of John's hands and went into prayer, praying for God's presence in John's life. He prayed for God's plan for John's life, asking for mercy and strength. John hadn't even known this man was a Christian.

For the next few months, they went through the roller coaster ride of cancer. John went through the entire Christmas season feeling blessed. "I am reading God's Word more than ever before. I'm really listening to God. I feel gratitude for everything this Christmas. I even noticed the smell of the Douglas Fir in my living room. I'm at complete peace."

We've been through two Christmases since this horrible news. Against all human odds, God healed John from the cancer. There is no trace of cancer cells in his body. He has a job he loves. He's grateful to be alive but no longer afraid of death. "I am grateful for everything that happened. My perspective on life has changed."

Application (5-10 Minutes)

Making It Personal

Christmas Day is almost here. Write a prayer asking God for an abundant Christmas for you and your family. Offer Him your circumstances and claim His promise of abundance, love, joy, and peace.

_____

_____

_____

_____

Praying Continuously (1 Thessalonians 5:17)

- Praise God throughout the day:
    - Praise Him when you see Christmas decorations.
    - Praise Him when you hear Christmas music.
    - Praise Him when you hear the word Christmas.

Ending The Day

- Did circumstances keep you from experiencing God's peace? If so, confess.
- Did your faith waver today? Did you doubt? If so, confess.
- Are you angry with anyone? If so, ask God to help you forgive.
- Praise God for the peace that is beyond understanding.

Christmas Worship

Meditation (3-5 Minutes)

Begin by being still before God. Meditate on the words "And Mary said, 'My soul doth magnify the Lord, and my spirit hath rejoiced in God my Saviour. For he hath regarded the low estate of his handmaiden: for, behold, from henceforth all generations shall call me blessed. For he that is mighty hath done to me great things; and holy is his name. And his mercy is on them that fear him from generation to generation. He hath shewed strength with his arm; he hath scattered the proud in the imagination of their hearts. He hath put down the mighty from their seats, and exalted them of low degree. He hath filled the hungry with good things; and the rich he hath sent empty away. He hath helped his servant Israel, in remembrance of his mercy; as he spake to our fathers, to Abraham, and to his seed forever.'" (Luke 1:46-55 KJV)

- Be still and know He is God.
- Let your soul glorify the Lord.
- Let your spirit rejoice in God your Savior.
- His mercy is available to all who fear him. Surrender to His mercy.
- He has performed mighty deeds with His arms. Surrender to His strength.
- He has brought down the proud and lifted the humble. Stand straight. You are the child of a King.
- He has blessed all descendents of Abraham. You are his descendent, adopted into His kingdom. Praise God.
- Listen to the voice of God.

Prayer (5-10 Minutes)

Appendix A: Requests of the Christ Child

- Ask God to speak to you during this devotional time.
- In Appendix A, ask God to teach you how to worship at a deeper level.
- Ask the Holy Spirit to fill you with the Christmas Spirit as you worship Him today.
- Update Appendix A with any other prayers and answers.
- Ask for knowledge of His will for you this Christmas and the power to carry it out.
- Ask the Holy Spirit to interpret the scriptures you are about to read.

Appendix B: Gifts from the Christ Child

- In Appendix B, list worshiping God as a blessing.

Appendix C: Gifts to the Christ Child

- Glorify God and sing Him your favorite Christmas carol.
- Kneel and offer your gifts listed in Appendix C in worship.
- Pray and update Appendix C. Just three more days until Christmas.

Appendix D: Celebrations for the Christ Child

- Turn to Appendix D and update your "To Do" list. Continue keeping this list no matter how busy you are.
- Enjoy your Christmas celebrations.

Bible Study (10-15 Minutes)

Do you worship Christmas or do you have Christmas worship? The busyness of the season tempts us to worship the season and leaves us with little time to worship the Christ Child. A dictionary's definition of worship includes words like reverent love and ardent devotion. It's interesting that love and devotion aren't enough. To count as worship, our love must be reverent and our devotion ardent.

As humans, we need to worship. There are signs of worship in most civilizations. Over the centuries, man has worshiped many things. Examples found throughout history include worship of statues, kings, the moon, the stars, the sun, women, cows, and gods with many names and shapes. Without guidance, our worship becomes pointless, unfocused, and even dangerous. History gives many accounts of worship gone awry.

To those of us who believe the Bible, the need to worship is no surprise. God created it and built us to need it. The question isn't "if" we worship, it is "who or what" we worship.

Christmas is a time for worship. People who worship no other time of the year worship at Christmas. The Bible doesn't define worship, but it does tell us whom to worship and makes suggestions for how to worship. We each have individual worship preferences based on cultural backgrounds, personality, and spiritual gifts. People with similar preferences naturally gravitate toward one another. As you study the worship of the ancients, compare your worship preferences. With whom do you identify?

Background Scripture

The Wise Men

Read Matthew 2:1-2. God leads true seekers to Jesus. The Wise Men were spiritual seekers and astrologers. They were the mystics of ancient time. Most likely, worship of the skies was part of their lifestyle. If the object of their worship had met their needs, they might not have sought the Christ Child. Our God of Wisdom used a star to get their attention. What title did the Wise Men give the child they were seeking? What did they want to do when they found him?

_____

_____

Read Matthew 2:3-6. One reality about truth is that it deeply disturbs those refusing to accept it. How did King Herod respond to their questions? Why do you think he took their questions seriously?

_____

_____

Read Matthew 2:7-8. Every religious practice has false worshippers. How did King Herod try to trick the Wise Men?

_____

_____

Read Matthew 2:9-10. What was the Wise Men's response to seeing the Christ Child? What form did their worship take?

_____

_____

Read Matthew 2:12. After seeing and worshiping the "Truth," the Wise Men had a new source of wisdom. Whose voice do you think warned them in the dream?

_____

_____

Mary

Read Luke 1:46-47. It is our privilege to witness a private worship service held by Mary and Elizabeth. Whom is Mary worshiping?

_____

_____

Read Luke 1:48. What is Mary's attitude during worship?

_____

_____

Zechariah

Read Luke 1:67-79. Zechariah is worshiping God while celebrating the birth of his son. Look at verse 67. The Holy Spirit filled Zechariah as he worshiped. What spiritual gift is Zechariah demonstrating in these verses?

_____

_____

List the praises Zechariah offered to God.

_____

_____

What prophecies did Zechariah make as he worshiped?

_____

_____

Angels

Read Luke 2:13-14. God gives us a glimpse of the Heavenly Host worshiping Him. Like Zechariah and Mary, they first gave glory to God. What prophecies did the angels make through their worship?

_____

_____

Shepherds

Read Luke 2:20 to see another aspect of worship. Like the others, the shepherds glorified and praised God. Then the shepherds left the Baby Jesus, went into the world, praising God as they went. For what did they praise Him? What impact do you think it had on the people they met?

_____

_____

Simeon

Read Luke 2:25. When we meet Simeon, he is waiting on the Lord. Describe his spiritual state. How is it similar to Zechariah's?

_____

_____

Read Luke 2:26. Simeon's spiritual preparation enabled him to hear God's voice. What promise had God made?

_____

_____

Read Luke 2:27. How was Simeon obedient with his personal worship?

_____

_____

Read Luke 2:28-32. Simeon saw the hand of God through his worship. What did God reveal?

_____

_____

How did Simeon demonstrate an eternal perspective through his worship?

_____

_____

Read Luke 2:33-35. Simeon also used prophecy in his worship. What prophecy did he give? How did Jesus' parents receive it?

_____

_____

Anna

Read Luke 2:37. God blessed Anna by calling her to full-time worship. How did she worship?

_____

_____

Read Luke 2:38. Like the others we studied, Anna gave thanks to God. She was also a prophetess. Who was the recipient of her message?

_____

_____

As we study these beautiful passages of worship, we notice trends. People are overjoyed and lift their voices in praise. Filled with gratitude, they shout their thanks to God. Filled with awe, they fall to their knees in worship. Peace enables them to face their future. We see gifts given to the Christ child and personal sacrifice through fasting. The Holy Spirit fills those who truly worship. Much of the Christmas worship included prophecies.

Actions follow worship. After Zechariah worshiped, he had a son to raise and a congregation to lead. After the Wise Men worshiped, they had the wisdom to avoid King Herod. After Mary worshiped with Elizabeth, she returned home to an uncertain future. Simeon was old and became willing to face impending death. The shepherds rose from worship ready to accept their mission. Anna spoke about the Christ child to all who would listen.

Mesa Verde

Humans are so imaginative they sometimes invent elaborate and even dangerous worship styles. Many religions have included sensuality and human sacrifices as a part of worship. People have a strong need for fairness that creates a need for sacrifice. Throughout history, most religions incorporate sacrifice of some kind into their worship practices. Often the sacrifices are of the innocent.

Anthropologists believe that in the 13th century, the Puebloans at Mesa Verde worshiped in something called the Sun Temple. Like the Wise Men, they studied the stars, sun, and moon. They watched the changing conditions. Their cliff-dwelling lifestyle depended on water. Being logical, they paid attention to the extraordinary astronomical events that took place when they had plenty of water. Droughts were disastrous for them. They watched for things like supernovae, sunspots, and eclipses to ensure water.

Being a spiritual society, they performed prayers or ceremonies to their gods in an effort to ensure that the good conditions repeated themselves. When the normal prayers and rituals were unsuccessful, the Puebloans sacrificed young women to appease their gods.

By nature, mankind is also superstitious. When prayers and rituals failed to bring the much-needed water, the Puebloans began looking for the cause. They suspected a witch lived among them, became suspicious of each other, and went on witch-hunts. They brutally executed many suspected witches.

After trying hard work, worship of false gods, prayer to false gods, human sacrifices, and murder, the Puebloans gave up and simply left their homes. They moved to another cliff in the same cold dry climate and started the process again. Is it true that "insanity is doing the same thing repeatedly, expecting different results"?

Application (5-10 Minutes)

Making It Personal

Take a worship style inventory.

- Do you begin by glorifying God? _____
- Do you feel the presence of the Holy Spirit? _____
- Do you fall to your knees (or some other act of reverence) in awe? _____
- Do you wait with anticipation on the Lord? _____
- Have you tried fasting? _____

- Do you shout or sing your praises to God? _____
- Do you lift your voices in thanksgiving? _____
- Do you easily give and/or receive prophecies (fresh words from God)? _____
- What else is part of your worship?

_____

- Whose worship style from the Christmas story most resembles your preferences? Why?

_____

Praying Continuously (1 Thessalonians 5:17)

- Worship God throughout your day.
- Stop and listen to the Christmas music. Hum in thanksgiving.
- When you see presents under your tree, offer them to the Christ Child in worship.
- Find a private time to kneel in awe.
- Glorify God to all who listen.
- Ask God to send you a fresh word from Him today.

Ending The Day

- Did you worship God today? If not, confess and ask for help.
- Did you experience wonder in your worship? If not, confess and ask for help.
- Did you hear the voice of God through your worship? If not, ask God to speak more clearly.
- Praise God for Christmas.

Memories of Christmas Past

Meditation (3-5 Minutes)

Begin by being still before God. Meditate on the words "Nay, in all these things we are more than conquerors through him that loved us. For I am persuaded, that neither death, nor life, nor angels, nor principalities, nor powers, nor things present, nor things to come, Nor height, nor depth, nor any other creature, shall be able to separate us from the love of God, which is in Christ Jesus our Lord." (Romans 8:37-39 KJV)

- Be still and know He is God.
- In all things, we can be conquerors through Him who loves us. Claim the promise and rejoice. Meditate on the following:
    - No matter whom we are missing this Christmas season, death can't separate us from the love of Jesus.
    - Life can't separate us from the love of Jesus.
    - Things present or things to come can't separate us from the love of Jesus.
    - No authority (boss, spouse, or other authority figure) can separate us from the love of Jesus.
    - Even angels can't separate us from the love of Jesus Christ.
- The Christmas Spirit is waiting. Enjoy it.
- Listen to the voice of God.

Prayer (5-10 Minutes)

Appendix A: Requests of the Christ Child

- Ask God to speak to you during this devotional time.
- For all things, there is a season. Is this Christmas a season of grief? Turn to Appendix A and ask God for comfort.
- Are you missing someone? In Appendix A, ask God to help create new memories for Christmas.
- Are you unsure if your deceased loved one is spending his or her eternity with God? In Appendix A, ask God for acceptance and peace.
- Update Appendix A with any new requests or answers.
- Ask for knowledge of His will for you this Christmas and the power to carry it out.
- Ask the Holy Spirit to interpret the scriptures you are about to read.

Appendix B: Gifts from the Christ Child

- Praise God that we have a home waiting for us in heaven.
- In Appendix B, list the names of loved ones in heaven.

Appendix C: Gifts to the Christ Child

- If you are grieving, offer God your heart to heal.
    - Offer Him your decision to count your blessings this Christmas.
    - Offer Him your determination to stay out of the pit of despair.
    - Offer Him your willingness to accept your assigned seasons of grief.
- Check Appendix C to make sure you are finished Christmas shopping and wrapping.

Appendix D: Celebrations for the Christ Child

- Tomorrow is Christmas Eve. Prayerfully prepare for it.
- Turn to Appendix D and update your "To Do" list.

Bible Study (10-15 Minutes)

Christmas is a time for memories and we often find ourselves remembering loved ones no longer with us. Grief, anger, loneliness, and self-pity threaten those sweet memories. If we aren't careful, happiness from our past will ruin our present.

For example, I loved going to Georgia to visit my grandparents for Christmas. Lying in the freezing bedroom under mounds of soft homemade quilts was part of the charm. As I sank into the soft mattress, waiting for Santa, I smelled the fresh pine of the walls and my grandmother's homemade biscuits. I remember standing around the piano, singing Christmas carols with them. At Christmas, I mentally walk through each room in their home, remembering the love and laughter.

I remember the first Christmas with my late son, David. He was only seven when he moved in and had never had a Christmas. He didn't understand the living room full of presents, and I have a sweet snapshot of a baffled child unable to comprehend the abundance before him. As I put his handmade ornaments on my tree, I ache as I surrender to the bittersweet memories.

Christmas is a time to remember and occasionally to grieve. The memories are both wonderful and painful. We turn to the Bible to learn how to put our memories in proper perspective.

Background Scripture

Read John 16:22. What is the promise?

_____

_____

Read Psalm 30:3. The Lord has chosen to keep us alive. Write the prayer in Psalm 30:3 and pray it repeatedly. The Lord can bring our souls up from the grave.

_____

_____

Read 1 Peter 4:12. Self-pity is a trap of Satan. If we want to have the Christmas spirit, we can't give in to self-pity. What are the instructions in the Scripture?

_____

_____

Read John 11:32-36. Grief is not a sin. Notice the demonstrations of grief by Mary and Jesus. Take the time to weep if necessary. The memories of Christmas are part of the healing process. Look at pictures and reminisce. Never feel guilty for grief. Jesus knew everything and yet He wept. Why do you think that was?

_____

_____

Read Joel 1:14. If grief is overwhelming, what should we do?

_____

_____

Read Psalm 116:15. As we grieve, we should never lose eternal perspective. What is God's perspective of death?

_____

Read Psalm 121:12. Satan wants grief to consume us and take away the joy of the season but we can stamp our foot and say no! Grief can be contained. After you look at pictures and cry, look up! Where does our help come from?

_____

_____

Read Galatians 6:2-3. This Christmas, make new memories with others. Let others help carry your burdens by allowing them to love you. What do you think it means, "In this way you will fulfill the law of Christ?"

_____

_____

Read Colossians 3:23. Throw yourself into having a wonderful Christmas. For whom are you doing it?

_____

_____

Read Philippians 4:13. "Impossible", you cry. "You do not understand who and/or what I have lost." Think again. What does the Scripture promise?

_____

_____

Read Colossians 3:15. This Christmas, be thankful, no matter what. Let the peace of Christ rule in your heart. God calls us to peace. Accept the call.

The Glad Game

By the time I met Vivian, she was already a widow. Elegantly beautiful, she always dresses regally, and I love it when she wears red. At church, she hugs me, tells me she loves me, and brags about my latest accomplishment. She signs all her correspondence, "Love, Love, Love."

Vivian is one of the hospitality leaders for our church. She stands at the front desk on Sunday greeting visitors and members. "Welcome," she says with a smile. "I'm so glad you came to Southside Baptist Church today." No one would dare doubt her sincerity.

Vivian was my first friend at Southside. At that time, she was director of the Sunday School for my age group. When I visited that first Sunday, I explained, "We love our church but have moved to this side of town. I'm not sure what God wants us to do."

"You belong at Southside," she said without hesitation. She wasn't taking no for an answer. Vivian, having the courage of her convictions, usually gets her way. She was right. We belonged at Southside.

Vivian is a faithful friend. She sat with me while my daughter Kelley was having a serious medical procedure. She won't allow her friends to doubt God. "She'll be fine," she insisted. Again, she was right. Kelley was fine. Vivian brought food when my grandmother died. In 1989, I stood in the hospital waiting room hearing that my husband's grandmother had terminal cancer. This was our third terminal illness in under a year and I was facing responsibility for much of her medical care. Tired and grieving two other recent deaths, I called Vivian crying, "I can't go through something else." I was in my last semester of getting my MBA, working full time, and had young children. How could I cope with another thing?

Vivian firmly snapped, "Yes, you can. You can do all things through Christ who strengthens you." As she said it, I felt my back straighten. Christ did give me the strength to get through that difficult time. I took care of Bob's grandmother as needed, made straight A's, and somehow kept my job. I even managed to help my children and husband deal with their grief. Only Christ could have made all of that possible.

I asked Vivian how she felt about Christmas. "I love Christmas," Vivian said. "I wear red for the entire month." She's active in our Women's Missions Union and makes sure our church takes care of missionaries at Christmas. She goes to every service the church offers.

You may be surprised that Vivian loves Christmas when you hear her story. She's a living example that one can really do all things through Christ. "I believe it is important to remain happy while here on earth. I refuse to let the circumstances of my life get me down," she said.

Vivian loved one man her entire life. That beloved husband died suddenly one Christmas morning. "I had to plan my husband's funeral while the gifts he bought me were still under the tree. I don't remember much about that morning, but I remember my pastor leaving his children's home and driving back to Jacksonville to be with me. Going back into church was hard. For years, we sat together in the same place every Sunday. We raised our two daughters and a son in Southside. Church made me think of my husband."

"If the memories were so strong, how could you go back?" I asked.

Startled by the question, she said, "The church is my home. You can't stop going to church. I made myself go every Sunday. In the beginning, I couldn't make myself sit in our place so I sat in the back of the church and left quickly afterward. Eventually, I began to love church again."

Vivian has other difficulties to grieve at Christmas. Her friends are beginning their journeys to eternity and she has to face Christmas without them. Her best friend was in a nursing home and no longer recognized Vivian. At the same time, I watched her go through an entire Christmas season with her son's health rapidly declining. She grew exhausted from caring for him but never lost her Christmas spirit. He died shortly after Christmas.

According to the great optimist Pollyanna, there are over 800 "Glad Passages" in the Bible. In the movie named for the main character, Pollyanna had just lost her parents and consequently had to move in with an aunt she had never met. Pollyanna's positive attitude helped an entire town to count their blessings by introducing the town to the "Glad Passages" in the Bible. There is a beautiful line in that movie where the preacher says, "If God said to be glad over 800 times, we should probably listen to Him."

In one particularly moving scene, Pollyanna describes the "Glad Game." She had wanted a doll for Christmas but her missionary parents were poor. Her father wrote to the missionary board about his daughter's request, but there was a mix up and she got crutches instead. She was disappointed so her father invented "The Glad Game." In "The Glad Game," you find something to be glad about, no matter what happens. Pollyanna decided to be "glad" that she didn't need the crutches.

Vivian plays the "Glad Game." If you ask about Christmas, she beams. "I love Christmas. I refuse to associate Christmas with anything other than the love of Christ and my blessings. God has blessed me so much."

"Is Christmas harder for you because your husband died on Christmas?" I asked.

Her answer: "Anyone who has lost someone precious certainly misses them on Christmas. I don't believe this day is any harder for me than for anyone else. I refuse to feel sorry for myself. I have too many blessings. I can't wait to visit my daughters and grandchildren on Christmas. I love my family and I love my church." When you ask about her son, she answers, "I'm grateful for a faithful daughter-in-law who took such good care of him while he was sick."

Vivian ended her Christmas story with, "My husband had been so sick before his death. I had a dream about him shortly after he died. In the dream, he was healthy and happy again. He was at a carnival, eating ice cream. I knew God was telling me how much better off he was. I rejoice in his happiness."

This Christmas, be grateful for the memories of Christmas Past and don't let those memories steal Christmas Present. Like Vivian, play the "Glad Game." Agree with Vivian and be happy while you're on this earth. Abraham Lincoln said most people are as happy as they make up their minds to be. This Christmas, be happy.

Application (5-10 Minutes)

Making It Personal

- Play the "Glad Game." List:
    - People you remember and miss.
    - Anything that is causing you pain or grief.
    - Write a reason to be glad about each item listed.

_____

_____

_____

_____

_____

_____

_____

_____

_____

- Are you grieving this Christmas?
    - Take time to grieve.
    - Allow no more than one hour each day.
    - Look at pictures.
    - Watch home videos.
    - Talk about the person.
    - Cry if it helps.
    - Arise from your grief and have an abundant Christmas.
    - Let others know that you are containing your grief to a specific time. Ask them not to talk about it other times.

- Take your thoughts captive and focus on what you have instead of what you lost.
- Determine to make new happy memories this Christmas.

Praying Continuously (1 Thessalonians 5:17)

- As you go through your day, play the "Glad Game."
  - When something upsets you, look for something to be glad about.
  - When something goes right, rejoice and be glad.
  - When you remember someone you lost, if appropriate, rejoice that they are with God.

Ending The Day

- Take a moment to remember "Christmas Past" and praise God for your memories.
- Praise God for the new memories He will give you this Christmas.
- If you spent today in the pit of despair, confess and ask for help.

Christmas Tips

Meditation (3-5 Minutes)

Begin by being still before God. Meditate on the words "Glory to God in the highest, and on earth peace, good will toward men." (Luke 2:14 KJV)

- Be still and know He is God.
- Give Glory to God in the highest.
- Sing the Christmas Carol "Angels We Have Heard On High."
- Meditate about peace on earth.
- Glory in the fact that God's good will rests on you.
- Listen to the voice of God.

Prayer (5-10 Minutes)

Appendix A: Requests of the Christ Child

- Ask God to speak to you during this devotional time.
- Ask God for peace:
    - As you worship Him today and tomorrow.
    - As you assess your Christmas celebrations.
- Ask God to help you accept the things you can't change.
- In Appendix A, ask God for wisdom:
    - To recognize His hand in Christmas.
    - To know what to change and what to accept.
    - To recognize the Christmas gifts He is sending you.

Appendix B: Gifts from the Christ Child

- Turn to Appendix B and thank God:
  - For Christmas Spirit.
  - For sending His son.
  - For the personalized Christmas Gift He is going to send you.
- Ask for knowledge of His will for you this Christmas and the power to carry it out.
- Ask the Holy Spirit to interpret the scriptures you are about to read.

Appendix C: Gifts to the Christ Child

- Wish the Christ Child a Merry Christmas.
- Ask Him if there is anything else He wants from you this Christmas.
- Turn to Appendix C one more time.

  Is there anything you need to do?

  Offer these gifts to Him in worship.

Appendix D: Celebrations for the Christ Child

- Turn to Appendix D and check your "To Do" list.
- Praise God that He is going to make your future Christmas celebrations even more meaningful.

Bible Study (10-15 Minutes)

As we listen to Christmas carols about Christmas being the most wonderful time of the year, we sigh at our inadequacy. We see pictures of the Norman Rockwell Christmas and wonder if this kind of Christmas is possible. Yet we keep longing for an abundant Christmas, with pockets full of the Spirit of Christmas.

All things are possible through Christ. Knowing what to do is simple, but doing it is hard. The simple part is looking at the Scripture and learning what to do. The difficult part is obedience. Obedience may mean changing long-time traditions and it probably means changing attitudes. In some cases, it can even mean changing where we spend Christmas. Christ never promised us that following Him would be easy. Below is a list of ten biblical Christmas tips that can enhance our Christmas celebrations.

Background Scripture

<u>**Tip One: Love God and Others**</u>

Read Mark 12:29-31. What is the most important commandment?

_____

_____

What is the second most important commandment?

_____

_____

<u>**Tip Two: Remember Christ**</u>

Read Matthew 2:2. Seek Christ out. Pay homage to Him. Make Him the center of all celebrations. This Christmas Eve, as you go through your last Christmas celebration, ask the same question as the Wise Men. What was that question?

_____

_____

Read Deuteronomy 4:9. The season is busy and it's easy to forget the reason for the season. Don't let the knowledge of Jesus slip from your heart. Parents and grandparents, you will probably be with your family. What is your sacred assignment?

_____

_____

<u>**Tip Three: Worship God**</u>

Read Exodus 34:14. Find a Christmas Eve service and worship in church. Bow down and worship as you give Christmas gifts. Worship Christ in the privacy of your home. How does God feel when we forget to worship Him?

_____

_____

Pocket Full of Christmas

Tip Four: Do Not Steal

Read Mark 10:19. When we put Christmas on credit, how are we stealing from our future? The gifts we give are for the Christ Child. Our recipients only receive them on behalf of Him. When we make them anything else, we steal from the Christ Child.

_____

_____

Tip Five: Do Not Judge How Others Celebrate Christmas

Read Matthew 7:5. Disapproving the Christmas celebrations of friends and family could ruin our holidays, with one exception: If you and your Christmas celebrations are perfect, you can judge. What do the scriptures say we have to do before we can clearly see the mistakes of others?

_____

_____

Tip Six: Do not Overindulge

Read Proverbs 23:1-3 carefully. Gluttonous celebrations are a serious offense. What is better than being given to gluttony?

_____

_____

Tip Seven: Watch What You Say

Read James 3:5-6. Practice self-control regardless of what others say or do to you. Don't start a forest fire with the spark of your tongue. What does this Scripture call our tongue?

_____

_____

Tip Eight: Remember to Pray

Read Ephesians 6:18. How are we to pray?

_____

_____

Read 1 Thessalonians 4:17. How often are we to pray?

_____

_____

Tip Nine: Confess and Make Amends As Necessary

Read Psalm 32:5. Christmas is a lot of pressure. Exhaustion causes grumpiness. Everyone makes mistakes. Confess and apologize quickly. What is God's attitude about confessed mistakes?

_____

_____

Tip Ten: Have True Godly Fellowship With One Another

Read 1 John 1:7. What is the secret of true fellowship?

_____

_____

Read Acts 2:42. To what are we supposed to be devoted?

_____

_____

True Confessions: A Walton Christmas

All definitions of the word *tradition* include passing something from generation to generation. Christmas celebrations don't become a tradition until the next generation repeats it. Some of our celebrations are worth repeating and turning into a tradition. Others aren't.

Over twenty years ago, I got honest about my Christmas celebrations. They were mostly about work and rewards. The work included buying gifts, cooking, wrapping, putting up decorations, cleaning house, and performing in Christmas musical productions. The rewards were eating and receiving gifts. Trust me when I tell you the rewards didn't equal the work.

When I saw pictures of a Norman Rockwell Christmas, I decided to set my standards higher. I wasn't sure my Christmas celebrations had any similarity to Norman Rockwell's depiction. Yes, I knew that Jesus was the reason for the season. I went to Sunday School and Church and we studied the Christmas Story. Unfortunately, the Christmas Story had little to do with my holiday preparations. As a result, we had none of the peace.

That particular Christmas, I had thirteen Christmas musical performances of some kind. All of them included the word Jesus but I don't remember any of them involving my personal worship. I remember practicing, and becoming frustrated with those who hadn't practiced. I noticed every mistake and none of the beauty.

Christmas gifts were on a credit card. There is too much freedom in using a credit card with a high limit. If I haven't budgeted and am using credit, it's easy to buy anything I want. The theory is, "If you can't afford it anyway, you might as well go for broke." I certainly was broke after Christmas.

Food was everywhere and I failed miserably at avoiding foods that weren't good for me. In fact, much of Christmas that year involved the sin of gluttony.

Opening gifts could have been the highlight of Christmas Day. Instead, I was too stuffed to enjoy it. The gifts I had gone into debt for were opened in under ten minutes and some of them broke before the day was over. I seriously suspected that most gifts people bought for me stayed within their budget. I felt cheated.

Others were as tense as I was. A family member spoke sharply and hurt my feelings. I went home and cried myself to sleep. There had to be a better way!

I took a personal inventory of my Christmas and myself and realized my motives for buying gifts included trying to win or keep people's love and affection. Instead of loving my neighbor as myself, I was trying to make sure my neighbor loved me. I realized that I was stealing from my future when I purchased gifts I couldn't afford. I wasn't thinking of Christmas gifts as gifts to the Christ Child.

I felt like a hypocrite. I used the word Jesus in my musical productions but had failed to worship. I didn't demonstrate the love of Jesus to those I was leading in worship and was too exhausted to enjoy the worship services I attended.

Thinking about the food was the worst. I thought the days of letting food be a god were behind me. Instead, I let overeating steal Christmas from me. I was too sluggish from overeating to experience the joy of the day. For me, overeating is truly like putting a knife to my throat.

I also realized with horror that I had not read the Christmas story to my children. They heard it in church but not in our home.

I thought about all the times I had snapped at people during the holidays. I probably deserved having my feelings hurt on Christmas December. I wondered how many forest fires I had started with my unruly tongue.

I knelt and asked God to help me do better. God's answer was to send a re-run of *The Walton's*, a television show about a relatively happy and godly family. I decided to give up on a Norman Rockwell Christmas and try having a Walton's Christmas.

The Walton family went to the woods to cut down a tree. That was going too far. I decided that we could at least make a celebration out of buying the tree. From that day forward, Bob and the kids went together to get the Christmas tree. On the Walton's, the husband and the children brought the tree home to present to Mother. Mother smiled and said, "It's the best tree ever." Every year afterwards, my family heard the words, "It's the best tree ever."

The Walton's made a party out of decorating the tree. What a wonderful idea. We started having a party. We decorated the tree together as we played Christmas music. We opened every ornament and discussed memories. We videotaped our party and at the end, we drank hot chocolate and watched the video. Sometimes we watched videos of past years. The work of decorating the Christmas tree suddenly had a purpose of family bonding.

I was being compulsive about my musical productions at Christmas. After praying, I dropped most of them. The ones I participate in, I do with my entire heart. I pray about them and prepare carefully. Now I have time to watch other people's musical productions at Christmas.

The next Christmas was when I realized that if I focus on Christ at Christmas, He gives me a customized Christmas gift. He probably did all along but I didn't notice. The Christmas after my revelations, Chris got a Bible. We read the Christmas story together from his new Bible and he accepted Christ on Christmas Eve. What a gift! Three years later, my daughter accepted Christ on Christmas Eve, reading from her first Bible. God has sent a special gift each year, some big and some small. I don't have room to write them all.

I decided that I wanted my children to remember spending a day of cooking with their mother. On Christmas Eve, the children and I began experimenting. The Christmas carols played all day. The first year, the dressing was green. What can I say? I'm not a cook. It was fun to make but we haven't repeated that recipe. We have spent every Christmas Eve since, cooking to carols.

We added some entertainment to our Christmas Eve. We ate, sang carols, and had a Christmas recital. We began taking a trip to look at lights. We even started having a worship service in our home. Thanks to one of Kelley's sweet Sunday School teachers, we have a precious tradition. We light a candle, turn off the lights, and read the Christmas Story by candlelight. Everyone takes a turn sharing about the year and what he or she is grateful for. Then, everyone prays. We top the evening off by reading "Twas the Night Before Christmas…"

I began giving gifts I could afford and the family still loves me. Somewhere along the way, I realized that I should be praying about gifts. Since gifts are really to the Christ Child, I asked Him what He wanted for Christmas. That may seem obvious but it was a great revelation to me. I discovered that if I pray about what to give, God sends ideas that both delight and match the budget.

I promised God not to let food take another Christmas from me. My God is a jealous God and food can't take precedence over God, even on Christmas. I have kept my promise. On Christmas, like any other day, I eat healthy food. I don't overeat. I learned the hard way to refrain from suggesting others do the same. Most people think pie and cakes are essential to Christmas.

In spite of the changes, our Christmases are not perfect and occasionally, new annoyances slip in. While wrapping gifts, I hear myself being bossy and trying to get people to hurry. My family has grown accustomed to our Walton Christmas and doesn't tolerate turning gift-wrapping into a job instead of a celebration and worship. Thank God, my family accepts apologies and we can start over.

They say confession is good for the soul. I have shared my personal struggles because I thought it might give someone hope. Christ did a mighty work in our home. Christmas is now a time of joy. My children are grown and have no memory of what I was like before I learned to put Christ in the center of Christmas.

Application (5-10 Minutes)

Making It Personal

- Look at Appendix D and do a Celebration Inventory.
    - Are your celebrations pleasant?
    - Do they point others to God?
    - Do they have a godly purpose?
    - Test them with "Ten Biblical Tips" above.
- Pray about each one and put a check mark by the ones worth repeating.
- What changes do you need to make for next year?

_____

_____

_____

_____

Praying Continuously (1 Thessalonians 5:17)

- As you go through the next two days, pay attention to your celebrations.
    - Notice how you feel while participating.
    - Praise God for the worthwhile traditions and other celebrations you experience.
    - Confess any that are not godly.
    - Ask God what He wants you to change next year.
- Look for the unique Christmas gift Christ is going to send you.

Ending The Day

- Review your day.
- Was your Christmas Eve worthy of the Christ Child? If not, confess.
- Ask Him what He wants from you on Christmas Day.
- Sing the Christmas Carol "Silent Night."

Christmas Presence

Meditation (3-5 Minutes)

Begin by being still before God. Meditate on the words "As the hart panteth after the water brooks, so panteth my soul after thee, O God. My soul thirsteth for God, for the living God: when shall I come and appear before God?" (Psalm 42:1-2 KJV)

- Be still and know He is God.
- Allow your soul to pant for God as a deer pants for water.
- Today, on Christmas Day, thirst for the living God.
- Listen to the voice of God.

Prayer (5-10 Minutes)

Appendix A: Requests of the Christ Child

- Ask God to speak to you during this devotional time.
- Oh God, the Father, Son, and Holy Ghost:
    - I praise your Holy Name and long for Your presence today.
    - Give me Your joy and power on this Holiest of Holy Days.
    - Take away difficulties so victory will be a witness to your power and love in my life.
- In Appendix A, ask God for a Merry Christmas for those around you.
- Ask for knowledge of His will for you this Christmas and the power to carry it out.
- Ask the Holy Spirit to interpret the scriptures you are about to read.

Appendix B: Gifts from the Christ Child

- Oh God, the Father, Son, and Holy Ghost:
    - I am still and feel your presence. Thank you.
    - I feel your love flowing through me and I have your peace.
    - You have made me worthy of your presence by the Gift you gave on the first Christmas.
- In Appendix B, thank God for sending the Gift.
- In Appendix B, thank God for His presence on Christmas Day.

Appendix C: Gifts to the Christ Child

- Oh God, the Father, Son, and Holy Ghost:
    - I offer myself to you to shape and to do with as you will.
    - I offer my gifts to you.
    - Use them as a witness to Your mighty power.
    - Bless them.
    - Use them to demonstrate Your love for the recipients.
    - Today, I will not be afraid to tell the world of your presence.
- Go to Appendix C and wish God a Merry Christmas as you recall each gift given.

Appendix D: Celebrations for the Christ Child

- Oh God, the Father, Son, and Holy Ghost:
    - This day is in celebration of Jesus Christ, my Lord and Savior.
    - I am ready. I put down my "To Do" list and celebrate.

Bible Study (10-15 Minutes)

The Jewish people knew for centuries that the Messiah was coming and yet most missed it. They were waiting and taught their children to look for Him. Jesus fulfilled all of the hundreds of prophecies they had studied and memorized. They became so angry and threatened over the possibility that He was the promised Gift that they crucified Him. Alas, even that was predicted and part of God's plan. Today, most Jews are still waiting for a Gift that has already come.

Today is Christmas. It is a day we have set aside for celebrating the Gift and yet many miss it. Today, as you go through your day, do not miss the Gift. Spend your day celebrating the Gift by filling your pockets with His presence. Look for the special gifts that the Gift has planned for you.

Background Scripture

Read Isaiah 7:14. God predicted the birth of Jesus centuries before He was born. What was the sign of the Christ Child?

_____

_____

Read Luke 1:26-27. How did God fulfill the prophecy from the book of Isaiah?

_____

_____

Read Micah 5:2. Where was the predicted birthplace of Jesus?

_____

_____

Read Matthew 2:1-2. How did God fulfill the prophecy from the book of Micah?

_____

_____

Read Jeremiah 31:15. What is Jeremiah predicting?

_____

_____

Read Matthew 2:16. How did God fulfill the prophecy from the book of Jeremiah?

_____

_____

Read Luke 2:38. Not everyone missed the Christmas Presence. Whom did Anna tell about the Christ child?

_____

_____

Read Matthew 2:2. Unexpected people recognized and worshiped the Gift. Who were they? Can you think of others that recognized the Christmas Presence?

_____

_____

Read Matthew 2:3-4. How did most people feel about the Gift?

_____

_____

Read Matthew 2:11. Today, join the Wise Men and bow down in worship. Open your Christmas presents and offer them to the Christmas Presence. If you ask and watch, Jesus will send you a special gift. Keep your eyes open. Don't miss your gift from The Gift.

Don't Forget The Baby

A young seminary student spent many of his student evenings gathered in a basement set aside for the recreation of those called to full-time Christian service. There with his friends, he laughed, played, and dreamed.

This young man finally graduated, and as expected, fell in love and married. He began preaching in his first church and was puzzling over his first Christmas sermon. Just before his first Christmas at this church, God delighted him and his wife as their first child was born. When the baby was just a few weeks old, his friends from seminary called. "We want to have a party and meet the baby. Let's do it back in the school basement."

This daddy was proud and excited but his wife was nervous about letting their helpless infant leave for an evening with a bunch of guys. "You haven't taken him off alone yet," she argued.

"We will be fine," daddy soothed.

As he arrived at the basement door, he heard laughter from inside. He walked into a room filled with friends, colorful balloons, a cake, and gifts for the child. His friends surrounded him as he and his son entered. They placed the young baby in the middle of the table and cooed with him. The father opened gifts and everyone except the baby ate cake. Eventually, the baby nodded off so they moved him over to a quiet corner of the room.

The years slipped away and for a short time, they became young seminary students again. They talked about old times as they played the games that had consumed so many of their hours. They caught up with each other's life and spun new dreams until the middle of the night. Finally, they realized how late it was and reluctantly stood up.

The young preacher boxed up the gifts and climbed the stairs with his friends. He made it all the way upstairs and out to his car before he remembered the baby. Heart pounding, he rushed back to the entrance, tore down the stairs to find his son still sleeping peacefully and unaware he had been forgotten.

As he got back in his car, his son nestled into the car seat, he smiled ruefully. Perhaps his wife's concern about him going off alone with the baby was valid. His son was the purpose of the party. He had accepted and opened the gifts on his son's behalf. He had even carried the gifts to the car but he had forgotten the baby. He knew he had his first Christmas sermon.

Application (5-10 Minutes)

Making It Personal

Write a birthday wish to Jesus, wishing Him a Merry Christmas. Offer Him your presents in worship. Ask for the Christmas Presence as you open your Christmas presents. Thank him for being the sacrificial Gift.

Dear Jesus:

_____

_____

_____

Love, _____

Praying Continuously (1 Thessalonians 5:17)

- Read the Christmas Story sometime during the day.
- As you go through your day, experience the Christmas Presence.
- Tell those who receive a present from you that it is in honor of the Christmas Presence.
- Look for the customized Christmas present the Christmas Presence will give you.

Ending The Day

- Thank God for His Presence and presents.
- Review Christmas Day:
    - Was it worthy of the Christmas Presence?
    - What changes do you need to make next year?
    - Confess if necessary.
- Sing "Away in a Manger" and whisper good night to Jesus.

Requests of the Christ Child (A Prayer List)

Instructions: Daily, date and name your prayer requests on the first line. On the second line date and record the answers (even if the answer is no or not right now.)

Date _____ Prayer Request _____

Date _____ Answer _____

Date _____ Prayer Request _____

Date _____ Answer _____

Date _____ Prayer Request _____

Date _____ Answer _____

Date _____ Prayer Request _____

Date _____ Answer _____

Date _____ Prayer Request _____

Date _____ Answer _____

Date _____ Prayer Request _____

Date _____ Answer _____

Date _____ Prayer Request _____
Date _____ Answer _____

Date _____ Prayer Request _____
Date _____ Answer _____

Date _____ Prayer Request _____
Date _____ Answer _____

Date _____ Prayer Request _____
Date _____ Answer _____

Date _____ Prayer Request _____
Date _____ Answer _____

Date _____ Prayer Request _____
Date _____ Answer _____

Date _____ Prayer Request _____
Date _____ Answer _____

Date _____ Prayer Request _____
Date _____ Answer _____

Date _____ Prayer Request _____
Date _____ Answer _____

Date _____ Prayer Request _____
Date _____ Answer _____

Requests of the Christ Child (A Prayer List)

Date _____ Prayer Request _____

Date _____ Answer _____

Date _____ Prayer Request _____

Date _____ Answer _____

Date _____ Prayer Request _____

Date _____ Answer _____

Date _____ Prayer Request _____

Date _____ Answer _____

Date _____ Prayer Request _____

Date _____ Answer _____

Date _____ Prayer Request _____

Date _____ Answer _____

Date _____ Prayer Request _____

Date _____ Answer _____

Date _____ Prayer Request _____

Date _____ Answer _____

Date _____ Prayer Request _____

Date _____ Answer _____

Date _____ Prayer Request _____

Date _____ Answer _____

Date _____ Prayer Request _____

Date _____ Answer _____

Date _____ Prayer Request _____

Date _____ Answer _____

Date _____ Prayer Request _____

Date _____ Answer _____

Date _____ Prayer Request _____

Date _____ Answer _____

Date _____ Prayer Request _____

Date _____ Answer _____

Date _____ Prayer Request _____

Date _____ Answer _____

Date _____ Prayer Request _____

Date _____ Answer _____

Date _____ Prayer Request _____

Date _____ Answer _____

Date _____ Prayer Request _____

Date _____ Answer _____

Date _____ Prayer Request _____

Date _____ Answer _____

Date _____ Prayer Request _____

Date _____ Answer _____

Date _____ Prayer Request _____

Date _____ Answer _____

Gifts from the Christ Child (A Gratitude List)

Instructions: Daily, date and name your blessings as instructed in each devotional.

Date _____ Blessing _____

Date _____ Blessing _____

Date _____ Blessing _____

Date _____ Blessing _____

Date _____ Blessing _____

Date _____ Blessing _____

Date _____ Blessing _____

Date _____ Blessing _____

Date _____ Blessing _____

Date _____ Blessing _____

Date _____ Blessing _____

Date _____ Blessing _____

Date _____ Blessing _____

Date _____ Blessing _____

Date _____ Blessing _____

Date _____ Blessing _____

Date _____ Blessing _____

Date _____ Blessing _____

Date _____ Blessing _____

Date _____ Blessing _____

Date _____ Blessing _____

Date _____ Blessing _____

Date _____ Blessing _____

Date _____ Blessing _____

Date _____ Blessing _____

Date _____ Blessing _____

Date _____ Blessing _____

Date _____ Blessing _____

Date _____ Blessing _____

Date _____ Blessing _____

Date _____ Blessing _____

Date _____ Blessing _____

Date _____ Blessing _____

Date _____ Blessing _____

Date _____ Blessing _____

Date _____ Blessing _____

Date _____ Blessing _____

Date _____ Blessing _____

Date _____ Blessing _____

Date _____ Blessing _____

Date _____ Blessing _____

Date _____ Blessing _____

Date _____ Blessing _____

Date _____ Blessing _____

Date _____ Blessing _____

Date _____ Blessing _____

Date _____ Blessing _____

Gifts from the Christ Child (A Gratitude List)

Date _____ Blessing _____

Date _____ Blessing _____

Date _____ Blessing _____

Date _____ Blessing _____

Date _____ Blessing _____

Date _____ Blessing _____

Date _____ Blessing _____

Date _____ Blessing _____

Date _____ Blessing _____

Date _____ Blessing _____

Date _____ Blessing _____

Date _____ Blessing _____

Date _____ Blessing _____

Date _____ Blessing _____

Date _____ Blessing _____

Date _____ Blessing _____

Date _____ Blessing _____

Date _____ Blessing _____

Date _____ Blessing _____

Date _____ Blessing _____

Date _____ Blessing _____

Date _____ Blessing _____

Date _____ Blessing _____

Date _____ Blessing _____

Date _____ Blessing _____

Date _____ Blessing _____

Date _____ Blessing _____

Date _____ Blessing _____

Date _____ Blessing _____

Date _____ Blessing _____

Date _____ Blessing _____

Date _____ Blessing _____

Date _____ Blessing _____

Date _____ Blessing _____

Date _____ Blessing _____

Date _____ Blessing _____

Date _____ Blessing _____

Date _____ Blessing _____

Date _____ Blessing _____

Date _____ Blessing _____

Date _____ Blessing _____

Date _____ Blessing _____

Date _____ Blessing _____

Date _____ Blessing _____

Date _____ Blessing _____

Date _____ Blessing _____

Date _____ Blessing _____

Date _____ Blessing _____

Date _____ Blessing _____

Date _____ Blessing _____

Date _____ Blessing _____

Date _____ Blessing _____

Date _____ Blessing _____

Date _____ Blessing _____

Date _____ Blessing _____

Date _____ Blessing _____

Date _____ Blessing _____

Date _____ Blessing _____

Date _____ Blessing _____

Date _____ Blessing _____

Gifts for the Christ Child (A Christmas Gift List)

Instructions:

Name: Write the name of the person accepting the gift on behalf of the Christ Child.

Gift Ideas: After praying, list gift ideas.

Budget $: Write the amount you can afford to spend.

Gift: Fill this in at the time of purchase or when the gift is complete.

Actual $: The actual amount spent—Note the difference from the actual budget amount.

Name _____ Gift Ideas _____
Budget $ _____ Gift _____ Actual $_____

Name _____ Gift Ideas _____
Budget $ _____ Gift _____ Actual $_____

Name _____ Gift Ideas _____
Budget $ _____ Gift _____ Actual $_____

Name _____ Gift Ideas _____
Budget $ _____ Gift _____ Actual $_____

Name _____ Gift Ideas _____
Budget $ _____ Gift _____ Actual $_____

Pocket Full of Christmas

Name _____ Gift Ideas _____
Budget $ _____ Gift _____ Actual $_____

Name _____ Gift Ideas _____
Budget $ _____ Gift _____ Actual $_____

Name _____ Gift Ideas _____
Budget $ _____ Gift _____ Actual $_____

Name _____ Gift Ideas _____
Budget $ _____ Gift _____ Actual $_____

Name _____ Gift Ideas _____
Budget $ _____ Gift _____ Actual $_____

Name _____ Gift Ideas _____
Budget $ _____ Gift _____ Actual $_____

Name _____ Gift Ideas _____
Budget $ _____ Gift _____ Actual $_____

Name _____ Gift Ideas _____
Budget $ _____ Gift _____ Actual $_____

Name _____ Gift Ideas _____
Budget $ _____ Gift _____ Actual $_____

Name _____ Gift Ideas _____
Budget $ _____ Gift _____ Actual $_____

Name _____ Gift Ideas _____
Budget $ _____ Gift _____ Actual $_____

Name _____ Gift Ideas _____
Budget $ _____ Gift _____ Actual $_____

Gifts for the Christ Child (A Christmas Gift List)

Name _____ Gift Ideas _____
Budget $ _____ Gift _____ Actual $_____

Name _____ Gift Ideas _____
Budget $ _____ Gift _____ Actual $_____

Name _____ Gift Ideas _____
Budget $ _____ Gift _____ Actual $_____

Name _____ Gift Ideas _____
Budget $ _____ Gift _____ Actual $_____

Name _____ Gift Ideas _____
Budget $ _____ Gift _____ Actual $_____

Name _____ Gift Ideas _____
Budget $ _____ Gift _____ Actual $_____

Name _____ Gift Ideas _____
Budget $ _____ Gift _____ Actual $_____

Name _____ Gift Ideas _____
Budget $ _____ Gift _____ Actual $_____

Name _____ Gift Ideas _____
Budget $ _____ Gift _____ Actual $_____

Name _____ Gift Ideas _____
Budget $ _____ Gift _____ Actual $_____

Name _____ Gift Ideas _____
Budget $ _____ Gift _____ Actual $_____

Name _____ Gift Ideas _____
Budget $ _____ Gift _____ Actual $_____

Name _____ Gift Ideas _____
Budget $ _____ Gift _____ Actual $_____

Pocket Full of Christmas

Name _____ Gift Ideas _____

Budget $ _____ Gift _____ Actual $_____

Name _____ Gift Ideas _____

Budget $ _____ Gift _____ Actual $_____

Name _____ Gift Ideas _____

Budget $ _____ Gift _____ Actual $_____

Name _____ Gift Ideas _____

Budget $ _____ Gift _____ Actual $_____

Name _____ Gift Ideas _____

Budget $ _____ Gift _____ Actual $_____

Name _____ Gift Ideas _____

Budget $ _____ Gift _____ Actual $_____

Name _____ Gift Ideas _____

Budget $ _____ Gift _____ Actual $_____

Name _____ Gift Ideas _____

Budget $ _____ Gift _____ Actual $_____

Name _____ Gift Ideas _____

Budget $ _____ Gift _____ Actual $_____

Name _____ Gift Ideas _____

Budget $ _____ Gift _____ Actual $_____

Name _____ Gift Ideas _____

Budget $ _____ Gift _____ Actual $_____

Celebrations for the Christ Child (A Christmas "To Do" List)

Instructions:

Event: List the Christmas Celebration you plan to attend, participate in, or host.

Date: The date of the event.

Tasks: Write tasks necessary to prepare for the event.

Date Due: The day the task needs to be completed.

Date Completed: When the task is complete—Note the difference between due and completion dates.

Event:_____ Date: _____

	Tasks	Date Due	Date Completed
1.	_____	___/_____	___/_____
2.	_____	___/_____	___/_____
3.	_____	___/_____	___/_____
4.	_____	___/_____	___/_____
5.	_____	___/_____	___/_____

Event:_____ Date: _____

	Tasks	Date Due	Date Completed
1.	_____	___/_____	___/_____
2.	_____	___/_____	___/_____
3.	_____	___/_____	___/_____
4.	_____	___/_____	___/_____
5.	_____	___/_____	___/_____

Pocket Full of Christmas

Event:_____ Date: _____

    Tasks   Date Due   Date Completed

1. _____ /_____ /_____

2. _____ /_____ /_____

3. _____ /_____ /_____

4. _____ /_____ /_____

5. _____ /_____ /_____

Event:_____ Date: _____

    Tasks   Date Due   Date Completed

1. _____ /_____ /_____

2. _____ /_____ /_____

3. _____ /_____ /_____

4. _____ /_____ /_____

5. _____ /_____ /_____

Event:_____ Date: _____

    Tasks   Date Due   Date Completed

1. _____ /_____ /_____

2. _____ /_____ /_____

3. _____ /_____ /_____

4. _____ /_____ /_____

5. _____ /_____ /_____

Event:_____ Date: _____

    Tasks   Date Due   Date Completed

1. _____ /_____ /_____

2. _____ /_____ /_____

3. _____ /_____ /_____

4. _____ /_____ /_____

5. _____ /_____ /_____

Celebrations for the Christ Child (A Christmas "To Do" List)

Event:_____ Date: _____

    Tasks   Date Due   Date Completed

1. _____/_____/_____

2. _____/_____/_____

3. _____/_____/_____

4. _____/_____/_____

5. _____/_____/_____

Event:_____ Date: _____

    Tasks   Date Due   Date Completed

1. _____/_____/_____

2. _____/_____/_____

3. _____/_____/_____

4. _____/_____/_____

5. _____/_____/_____

Event:_____ Date: _____

    Tasks   Date Due   Date Completed

1. _____/_____/_____

2. _____/_____/_____

3. _____/_____/_____

4. _____/_____/_____

5. _____/_____/_____

Event:_____ Date: _____

    Tasks   Date Due   Date Completed

1. _____/_____/_____

2. _____/_____/_____

3. _____/_____/_____

4. _____/_____/_____

5. _____/_____/_____

Pocket Full of Christmas

Event:_____ Date: _____

    Tasks   Date Due   Date Completed

1. _____/_____/_____
2. _____/_____/_____
3. _____/_____/_____
4. _____/_____/_____
5. _____/_____/_____

Event:_____ Date: _____

    Tasks   Date Due   Date Completed

1. _____/_____/_____
2. _____/_____/_____
3. _____/_____/_____
4. _____/_____/_____
5. _____/_____/_____

Event:_____ Date: _____

    Tasks   Date Due   Date Completed

1. _____/_____/_____
2. _____/_____/_____
3. _____/_____/_____
4. _____/_____/_____
5. _____/_____/_____

Event:_____ Date: _____

    Tasks   Date Due   Date Completed

1. _____/_____/_____
2. _____/_____/_____
3. _____/_____/_____
4. _____/_____/_____
5. _____/_____/_____

To order additional copies of

Pocket Full of
Christmas

Have your credit card ready and call:

1-877-421-READ (7323)

or please visit our web site at
www.pleasantword.com

Also available at:
www.pocketfullofquarters.com
www.amazon.com
www.barnesandnoble.com

The author, Cheryle M. Touchton, would be honored to speak at your church
or organization. To contact her, call 1-904-821-5207
or e-mail Cheryle@pocketfullofquarters.com

Printed in the United States
54166LVS00002B/149-206